Change-mals

Expanding the *Change-mapping* tool-set

"I warmly recommend this book to change agents who are searching for a pragmatic change method and tools that make their impact felt immediately. I am sure you will find the tools and ideas presented valuable and gracefully challenging conventional practices. I wish I had known some of these tools much sooner in my career."
Jörg Schreiner,
Managing partner co-shift, Germany

""...Tom Graves shows us a set of tools that, when combined with the easy to follow structure for Change Mapping in the first book in this series, provides anyone in a change effort the ability to navigate uncertainty, and find answers to the most challenging problems. Perhaps not as apparent is the recursive, scalable and extensible nature of the material. Able to be used at every scale, and extended to accommodate any existing tools, the Change-Mapping approach set out in this series creates a consistent and reliable way of identifying real issues in organisations, and helping participants collaborate effectively in their resolution."
Darryl Carr
Enterprise Architect
Editor, Enterprise Architecture Professional Journal

Tom Graves with Joseph Chittenden

Copyright © 2021 Tom Graves and Joseph Chittenden

All rights reserved. No part of this publication *(apart from the blank tool-sheets)* may be reproduced, distributed, or transmitted in any form or by any means, including photocopying, recording, or other electronic or mechanical methods, without the prior written permission of the publisher, except in the case of brief quotations embodied in critical reviews and certain other non-commercial uses permitted by copyright law. For permission requests, write to the publisher, addressed "Attention: Permissions Coordinator," at the address below.

Published by
Tetradian Books
Unit 215
Communications House
9 St Johns Street
Colchester
Essex
CO2 7NN
England

http://www.tetradianbooks.com

First published March 2021
ISBN 978-1-906681-42-5 (Paperback)
ISBN 978-1-906681-43-2 (Ebook)
First Edition

Legal disclaimer

This book is presented solely for educational purposes. The authors and publisher are not offering it as legal, accounting, or other professional services advice. While best efforts have been used in preparing this book, the authors and publisher make no representations or warranties of any kind and assume no liabilities of any kind with respect to the accuracy or completeness of the contents and specifically disclaim any implied warranties of merchantability or fitness of use for a particular purpose. Neither the authors nor the publisher shall be held liable or responsible to any person or entity with respect to any loss or incidental or consequential damages caused, or alleged to have been caused, directly or indirectly, by the information contained herein.

Change-mapping tools

Expanding the *Change-mapping* tool-set

Tom Graves with Joseph Chittenden

Contents

i Preface

ii A big thank you! / About the author and the designer

iii What is *Change-mapping*?

iv What is a *Change-mapping* tool?

v A brief guide to using the tools

Part 1: The *Change-mapping* tools in action

4 Chapter 1 Big picture scenarios *(Context folder tools in action)*

6 How to measure value (*Value* tool)

10 How to proceed with limited information (*Sense-making* tool)

14 How to define an organisation (*Visioning* tool)

18 How to map an organisation's services (*Enterprise Canvas* tool)

22 How to rationalise a supply chain (*Holomap* tool)

26 How to guide an organisation (*Guide* tool)

30 How to see the customer's journey (*Service cycle* tool)

34 How to be effective (*Effectiveness* tool)

38 Chapter 2 People issues scenarios *(Scope folder tools in action)*

40 How to map how an organisation functions (*Inside/Out* tool)

44 How to resolve rapidly changing issues (*Decision* tool)

48 How to define leadership requirements (*Leadership* tool)

52 How to build a skilled team (*Skills learning* tool)

56 How to have a balanced team (*Modes* tool)

60 How to find what is really happening (*SEMPER* tool)

64 How to find the story of an organisation (*NOTES* tool)

68 How to prepare for unexpected knock-on effects (*Knock-on effects* tool)

72 Chapter 3 Planning scenarios *(Plan folder tools in action)*

74 How to map an organisation's capabilities (*SCORE* tool)

78 How to resolve an unknown issue (*Where to start?* tool)

82 How to reduce uncertainty (*SCAN* tool)

86 How to choose a new tool (*Tool finder* tool)

Part 2: Getting more out of *Change-mapping*

90 Chapter 4 How to run a Linked mission
92 A Linked mission using all the Tetradian tools *(part 1)*
94 A Linked mission using all the Tetradian tools *(part 2)*
96 A Linked mission using all the Tetradian tools *(part 3)*
98 A Linked mission using all the Tetradian tools *(part 4)*

100 Chapter 5 Getting more out of *Change-mapping*
102 Using the tool in different scenarios
104 Adapting the tools to your needs
106 Choosing which external tools to use
110 What's next in *Change-mapping*?
111 Other books by the author
112 Glossary

Preface
Expanding the tool-set

In the first *Change-mapping* book we set out to show what *Change-mapping* is and what it can do for organisations.
But it was a balance between too complex and too simple.
We decided to split the material into three books, one purely about how to learn the basics, one about the tools and one about more complicated uses of *Change-mapping*.
This book introduces twenty new tools which extend the power of *Change-mapping* while still being easy to use.
We wanted to show the tools in action, so we chose a set of scenarios which give a good sense of when and how to use each tool. Each page-spread uses a real world example as well as clear instructions about how to use the tool.
Another aim was to show how other tools such as *GANTT* charts can be used with *Change-mapping*, so there is a small section which shows some of these tools in use.
For each scenario we have illustrations created for this book, which help keep the tools grounded in the real world, as the ultimate aim of this book is to provide tools to help explore, address and resolve real world issues.

Photograph source: Flickr, Mike McBey. CGI Train, Joseph Chittenden

Tom Graves
Bendigo, Australia
March 2021

A big thank you!
To our co-creators and valued patrons

This book would not have existed without all of the people who over the years have helped to bring Change-mapping to a wider audience.
The author would like to thank, amongst others:
Michael Smith (Mexico)
Helena Read (Australia)

Patrons
The author would also like to thank all the valued Patrons at *www.patreon.com/tetradian* who helped fund the production of this book.
They have also given excellent feedback and helped with testing the materials.

How you can get involved!
To find out more about Change-mapping visit:
www.changemappingbook.com

If you would like to be involved with the development of new tools, testing and more then head over to Patreon to get involved.
www.patreon.com/tetradian

About the author
Tom Graves

Tom is known as a highly innovative thought leader on the futures of business. With a keen eye for systems and structure, he has nearly 40 years experience in knowledge management, skills research and software development.
He is a prolific author, and experienced presenter on radio and television, at conferences and in workshops and seminars.
Contact: info@tetradian.com

About the designer
Joseph Chittenden

Joseph has produced concepts and visuals for companies such as: *Tesco, Lotus sports cars, T-Mobile, Honda, Makita, UK Cabinet Office, Superdrug/3Phones*, and others on behalf of design agencies in England and Dubai.
www.jc3dvis.co.uk

What is *Change-mapping*?
A quick overview

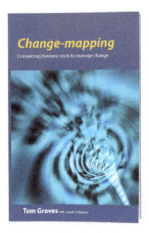

The first *Change-mapping* book
Inside the first book you learn how to run *Change-mapping* missions, see it in action, avoid common problems and how to run larger and more complex missions. There is also a complete set of basic tools to help you learn how to use *Change-mapping*.
It is available on Amazon and other book retailers.
ISBN 978-1-906681-40-1

This book is the follow-on to the *Change-mapping* book *(see left)*. It is recommended to have read that book before reading this one.

What happens if you have an issue which needs to be resolved? A typical response is to plan how to resolve the issue and then resolve it. While this is fine in principle, it can miss out vital steps, such as *'Why does the issue need solving?'* or *'Is this the best way to resolve the issue?' Change-mapping* is used to answer these types of questions. It does this by using a simple map system which breaks down any issue into manageable parts, as shown below.

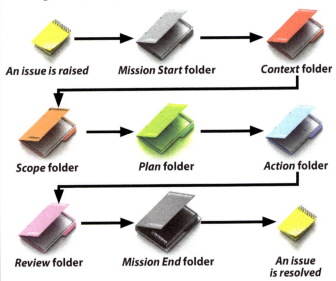

All these parts make up a **mission** to explore or resolve an issue. Every **mission** is run by a small team who are assisted by a **Pathfinder** who keeps the mission on track and an **Observer** who records all that is found.
When running a **mission** the team use tools to gather ideas, information and insights. How the tools work is discussed on the next page.

What is a *Change-mapping* tool?
Gathering ideas, information and insights

Within the first *Change-mapping* book was a set of basic tools which were deliberately simplified, so that you would not be daunted when first learning how to use them.

Once you became familiar with how the tools worked, then you would want to tackle more complex issues. There the basic tools would show their limits and the need for more sophisticated tools would be highlighted.

This book introduces twenty new *Change-mapping* tools which significantly expand *Change-mapping's* capabilities. The new tools are split into eight **Context folder** tools, eight **Scope folder** tools and four **Plan folder** tools. These tools are used within their respective folders in the same way as for the basic tools. For example you might use the **Value** tool *(see page 6)* in the **Context** folder.

What is an enterprise?
The word *'enterprise'* is mentioned throughout this book.
An organisation is *part* of an enterprise but it is not *the* enterprise.
If we imagine a copper mine, their enterprise is to mine copper. Mining the copper involves a huge amount of individual issues which need to be resolved.
This continual resolving of issues *is* the enterprise.
Inside the enterprise will be the organisation, suppliers, customers, equipment and much more.
For more information see *www.slideshare.net/tetradian/the-enterprise-is-the-story/*

Context folder　　　　　　*Scope* folder

Scenarios allow you to see how the tool would typically be used. For example the **Value** tool is shown being used to value ancient Chinese statues. Note though that any tool can be used within any scenario. For example the **Value** tool could be used to find out what is valued when moving copper mine trucks in Namibia *(see page 82)*.

So read through the scenarios to see what the tools are used for and then use them in your missions!

A brief guide to using the new tools

A simple scenario showing some of the new tools in action

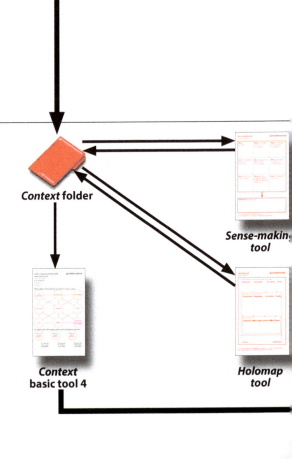

In this scenario a skills shortage issue has been raised by truck drivers, and articles on the internet. So an Australian logistics company decides to find out **why** there is a skills shortage **before** trying to change the situation.

The issue is 'a skills shortage in the logistics industry'.

Photograph source: Flickr, Prince Roy. CGI Truck from Turbosquid

The company used the **Mission Start** folder to set up the mission. The first tool used was the **Mission Start basic tool 1** *(See page 64 in the first Change-mapping book)* to establish **which** issue would be explored. Once a team was set up then they used the **Context** folder. The folder is closed to show when it is completed.

Mission Start folder

Mission Start basic tool 1

In the **Context** folder the team used the **Sense-making** tool *(See page 10)* to find out more about the issue. From a brief look on the internet they find that many of the truckers are due to retire and the tough working conditions are not attracting new recruits. They also use the **Holomap** tool *(See page 22)* to understand who are the stakeholders affected by the issue. They use the **Context basic tool 4** *(See page 64 in the first Change-mapping book)* to decide what to do next.

Context folder

Context basic tool 4

Sense-making tool

Holomap tool

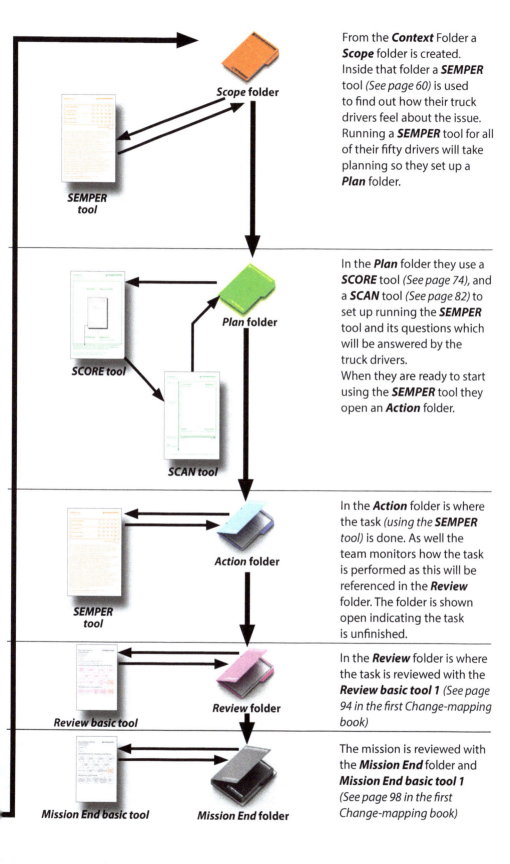

SEMPER tool	**Scope folder**	From the **Context** Folder a **Scope** folder is created. Inside that folder a **SEMPER** tool *(See page 60)* is used to find out how their truck drivers feel about the issue. Running a **SEMPER** tool for all of their fifty drivers will take planning so they set up a **Plan** folder.
SCORE tool / **SCAN tool**	**Plan folder**	In the **Plan** folder they use a **SCORE** tool *(See page 74)*, and a **SCAN** tool *(See page 82)* to set up running the **SEMPER** tool and its questions which will be answered by the truck drivers. When they are ready to start using the **SEMPER** tool they open an **Action** folder.
SEMPER tool	**Action folder**	In the **Action** folder is where the task *(using the SEMPER tool)* is done. As well the team monitors how the task is performed as this will be referenced in the **Review** folder. The folder is shown open indicating the task is unfinished.
Review basic tool	**Review folder**	In the **Review** folder is where the task is reviewed with the **Review basic tool 1** *(See page 94 in the first Change-mapping book)*
Mission End basic tool	**Mission End folder**	The mission is reviewed with the **Mission End** folder and **Mission End basic tool 1** *(See page 98 in the first Change-mapping book)*

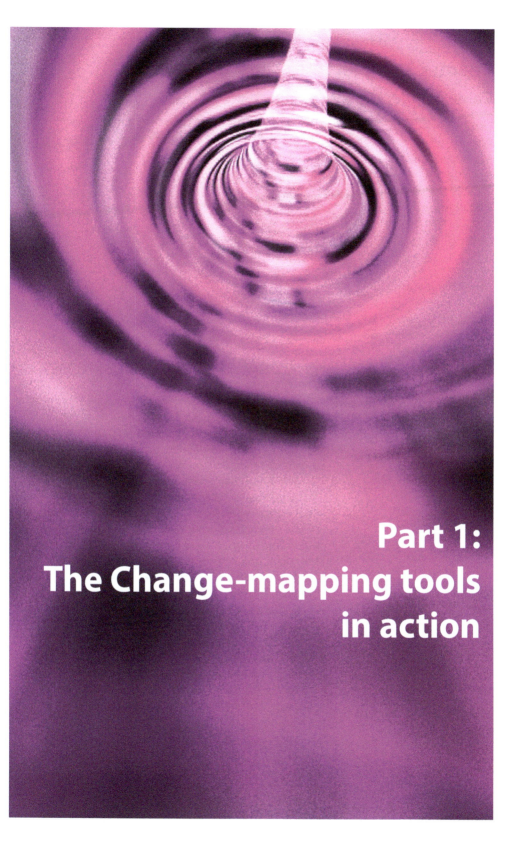

Chapter 1: Big Picture scenarios

Context folder tools in action

NOTE
All the scenarios are hypothetical and fiction. The organisations mentioned are used to illustrate a specific issue to better describe how the tools could be used.

Downloadable tools
Available at the time of writing to download are PDFs and PowerPoint slides of the tools shown in this chapter.
https://www.changemappingbook.com/context-tools

About these tools

In this chapter we look at tools used to explore the context of an issue or enterprise.

In the first *Change-mapping* book a simple **Context** tool was used, here we look at eight new **Context** tools. These tools allow much more context information to be found.

The tools in this chapter are used to:
• Measure the value of a product or service.
• Establish strategies for making sense of an unknown issue.
• Define an organisation's future.
• Map an organisation's services.
• Map the stakeholders within an issue.
• Guide how an organisation resolves issues.
• Understand an organisation's service cycle.
• Look at issues from a long term perspective.

The scenarios

In order to show how these new **Context** tools work, we have created eight scenarios. Each scenario has a real world issue which uses one of the tools to explore, address or resolve the issue.

It is important to note that any of the tools could be used in any scenario and are not limited to only being used within that specific scenario.

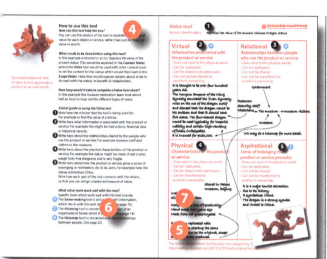

Using these tools in a Change-mapping mission

1. Set up a mission to explore or resolve an issue, with a *Mission start folder*.

2. Use a *Context folder* to explore the context of the issue. If the basic Context folder doesn't generate enough information, add one of the tools from this chapter, which best fits your requirements.

3. If the tool generates enough information then move to the *Scope folder*.

How to use this chapter

How can these tools help you?

These tools are used to explore the context (or big-picture) of an issue or enterprise. This will be vital when resolving issues by fully understanding the 'why' of an issue.

What needs to be done before using these tools?

You should read the first *Change-mapping* book, as this will show you how everything works and how to add more detailed tools, such as the ones shown in this chapter.

A brief guide to using this chapter
Each tool is discussed over four pages

A scenario showing the *Change-mapping* tool in use exploring a real world issue.

A general description of the tool discussing when and what it is used for.

A blank version of the tool which can be copied and used in your own *Change-mapping* missions.

Instructions showing how to use each tool including what needs to be done *before* using the tool.

A link to where you can find out more information online about the tool.

A list of other tools in the book which work well with the tool shown.

A filled-in example of the tool which uses the scenario to help you understand how to use the tool.

6. Big Picture scenarios

How to measure value
The Value Tool

CGI Model from Turbosquid

The scenario
In this imagined scenario, the Palace Museum in Beijing, China has a statue that is starting to degrade after hundreds of years. The museum's restoration team uses a **Value** tool to create a balanced value appraisal of the statue, which can be used to decide what to do next to benefit all stakeholders.

About this tool
A common way to value a product or service is to ask if it is worth a certain amount of money, is it *'good value'*?
But if something is only measured in financial terms, then we are missing its **true** value.
This version of the tool splits value into four parts:
Virtual (such as information), **Relational** (such as the connections between people who use the product or service), **Physical** (such as size or weight) and **Aspirational** (such as a product or service's brand).
The tool asks you to take your product or service and assign value in these four ways, but how can that help you?
The example we use here *(the red dragon statue)* shows that if we were to only consider the insurance value of the statue, we might be tempted to sell it. But doing that we would lose a priceless link to the past and something which is uniquely Chinese. The tool highlights the *less obvious* markers of value, so that you will obtain a more balanced view.
These values are often referred to, in many of the other tools in this book. Knowing the true value of a product or service will logically influence our decisions about whether they need to be kept as they are or changed.

About this tool in brief
Often a product or service is valued in only financial terms. This version of the tool helps you to measure the value of a product or service in four ways, to allow for a more balanced view.

More detail
With each part of the tool it can be useful to know:
Where is each part stored, eg the information is stored online, while the statue is in a museum.
When is it used, eg the statue's information is used during restoration.
How is it stored, eg the information about the statue is stored in a server in Shanghai while the statue is stored in a museum display in Beijing.
Who can access, eg does anyone need permission to access the information about the statue.

Value tool
Mission identification:

Virtual
Information associated with the product or service
- Does not exist in the physical world.
- Can be replicated.
- Can be shared with permission.
- Can not be transferred to another's ownership.

Relational
Relationships between people who use the product or service
- Does exist in the physical world.
- Can be replicated.
- Can not be shared.
- Can not be transferred to another's ownership.

Physical
Characteristics of the product or service
- Does exist in the physical world.
- Can be replicated.
- Can be shared with permission.
- Can be transferred to another's ownership.

Aspirational
Sense of belonging the product or service provides
- Does not exist in the physical world.
- Can be replicated.
- Can not be shared.
- Can not be transferred to another's ownership.

This tool is adapted from the Tetradian tool designed by Tom Graves
http://weblog.tetradian.com/2013/12/31/crud-crude-action-acronyms/

You need a balanced view of value to truly appreciate a product or service's worth.

How to use this tool

How can this tool help you?
You can use this version of the tool to establish four types of value for each object or service, rather than just its financial value or worth.

What needs to be done before using this tool?
In this example a mission is run to: *'Appraise the value of the ancient statue.'* This would be explored in the **Context folder**, where the **Value** tool would be used with other context tools to set the context for the statue which would then lead to the **Scope folder**. Here they would explore options about what to do next with the statue, to benefit all stakeholders.

How long would it take to complete a Value tool-sheet?
In this example the museum restoration team took about half an hour to map out the different types of value.

A brief guide to using the Value tool

❶ Note here the mission that the tool is being used for. For example to find the value of a statue.

❷ Write here what information is associated with the product or service. For example this might be instructions, financial data or historical records.

❸ Write here about the relationships shared by the people who use the product or service. For example museum staff and visitors to the museum.

❹ Write here about the physical characteristics of the product or service. For example the statue might be made of red crystal, weighs forty-five kilograms and is very fragile.

❺ Write here about how the product or service gives a sense of belonging or motivation, etc to its users. For example how the statue symbolises China.

Note how each part of the tool connects with the others, so that you can assign a balanced measure of value.

What other tools work well with this tool?
Specific tools which work well with this tool include:

Π The **Sense-making** tool is concerned with information, which ties in with this part of the tool. *(See page 10).*

Σ The **Visioning** tool is concerned with a vision of an organisation's future which it aspires to. *(See page 14).*

Φ The **Holomap** tool is concerned with the relationships between people. *(See page 22).*

Value tool

Mission identification: Appraise the value of the ancient Chinese Dragon statue

Virtual ② Π
Information associated with the product or service
- Does not exist in the physical world.
- Can be replicated.
- Can be shared with permission.
- Can not be transferred to another's ownership.

It is thought to be over four hundred years old.
The Hongwu Emperor of the Ming dynasty emulated the Yuan dynasty rules on the use of the dragon motif and decreed that the dragon would be his emblem and that it should have five claws. The four-clawed dragon would be used typically for imperial nobility and certain high-ranking officials. (Wikipedia).
It is insured for ¥180,000.

Relational ③ Φ
Relationships between people who use the product or service
- Does exist in the physical world.
- Can be replicated.
- Can not be shared.
- Can not be transferred to another's ownership.

Government
Restorers
Security staff
Historians → The museum → museum visitors
Investors

We may do a Holomap for more detail.

Physical ④
Characteristics of the product or service
- Does exist in the physical world.
- Can be replicated.
- Can be shared with permission.
- Can be transferred to another's ownership.

Stored in Palace museum, Beijing

Weight 45kg
Size 20 x 45 x 5cm

Designed as a one off-production
Hand made 400 years ago
Made from red glass/crystal

It has been replicated with many copies sharing the same characteristics as the original, except they were mass produced.

Aspirational ⑤ Σ
Sense of belonging the product or service provides
- Does not exist in the physical world.
- Can be replicated.
- Can not be shared.
- Can not be transferred to another's ownership.

It is a major tourist attraction due to its history.
It symbolises China.
The dragon is a strong symbol and linked to China.

This tool is adapted from the Tetradian tool designed by T
http://weblog.tetradian.com/2013/12/31/crud-crude-action-acronyms/

10. *People issues scenarios*

How to proceed with limited information
The Sense-making tool

CGI warehouse, Joseph Chittenden

About this tool in brief
Before trying to resolve an issue you need to know what the issue is, why does it happen and so on.
Once you know this you will be better placed to resolve it, which is what this version of the **Sense-making** tool does.

The scenario
In this imagined scenario a government department has misplaced important meteorological data, archived fifty years ago. Before trying to resolve the issue they want to find out more about the issue. They decide to use the **Sense-making** tool to better understand the why, how, when, what, where of the issue, to make sure they resolve the right issue.

About this tool
It could be argued that the most important information needed when resolving an issue is 'What is the issue?'
How can an issue be resolved if we don't know what the issue is or if it even needs resolving?
The **Sense-making** tool is used to describe what an issue is. If the issue is not fully understood, then any solution is likely to resolve the wrong thing. So this tool is used to orient an organisation in a more effective direction rather than just guessing what the issue is.
The tool uses a set of questions to build up a picture of what the issue is, when it is happening, who it affects and so on.
In our example of a government department, they find that misplaced data is the result of a change in computer systems sometime in the last fifty years. But the staff who were involved retired twenty years ago.
Now the issue has been described in more detail, the archive team can run missions to find the actual data they require. The information found in this tool will be used to inform what to do next. This is an important difference between exploring an issue and resolving an issue. Logically an issue can't be resolved without exploring what the issue is.

Sense-making tool

Mission identification:

What is the issue?	**When** is it thought the issue occurs or occurred?	**Where** is it thought the issue occurs or occurred?
How is it thought the issue occurs or occurred?	**Who** is thought to be affected by the issue occurring?	**What** is it thought to cause the issue occurring?
Why does the issue need resolving?	**What** apart from people is thought to be affected when the issue occurs?	**Why** is it thought the issue occurs?

Statement about the issue:

This tool is adapted from a blog by Tom Graves:
http://weblog.tetradian.com/2018/03/14/sensemaking-into-the-void/

You need to understand the issue before trying to resolve the issue.

How to use this tool

How can this tool help you?
This version of the tool is used to provide a quick overview of the issue so that the your organisation can then orient itself to best resolve it.

What needs to be done before using this tool?
In this example a mission is run to *'Find the misplaced meteorological data.'* So a small team using the standard *Change-mapping* system will run a mission to find the data. Using the **Sense-making** tool the team should better understand the context of the issue, knowing fully what is happening, before trying to change it with potentially unforeseen consequences. *(Unforeseen consequences are explored in the **Knock-on effects** tool, see page 68).*

A brief guide to using the Sense-making tool

❶ Note here the mission that the tool is being used for. For example to find misplaced meteorological data.

❷ In this part of the tool use the boxes to define the issue. Often, by describing the issue, it can be found that what is assumed to be causing the issue actually isn't at all. This will prove vital later, as any solution based on an incorrect assumption is likely to fail.
In this example they find that the issue actually occurred decades before.

❸ Here a summary of what was found in the boxes is noted. This will form the foundation of any solution that will be proposed. The **Sense-making** tool is meant to be used to give a quick appraisal of the issue before rushing to solve it. Another point to note is that it is not meant to be just a list filling exercise, but also to observe how the boxes *connect* with each other, which can highlight further insights.

What other tools work well with this tool?
As the tools in this book are trying to explore, address or resolve issues, knowing what the issue is has obvious benefits.

Π The **Holomap** tool can be used to define who is affected by the issue. *(See page 22).*

Σ The **Knock-on effects** tool looks at the consequences of action or inaction, which can be useful to know when considering if the issue needs resolving. *(See page 68).*

Sense-making tool ❶

Mission identification: **Find misplaced government weather records**

What is the issue? ❷	**When** is it thought the issue occurs or occurred?	**Where** is it thought the issue occurs or occurred?
Important weather records about floods have been misplaced and are needed to predict future floods.	Sometime within the last fifty years, possibly when the archives were moved from the old archive.	Within the archive and also the archive record which doesn't match the actual archive.
How is it thought the issue occurs or occurred?	**Who** is thought to be affected by the issue occurring? ⊓	**What** is it thought to cause the issue occurring?
The archive record must have not been properly updated at some point.	The meteorological department needs data to build accurate forecasting models.	A mismatch between archive records and the actual records. An older computer system nobody now uses?
Why does the issue need resolving? Σ	**What** apart from people is thought to be affected when the issue occurs?	**Why** is it thought the issue occurs?
The meteorological models need more old data to show long-term weather trends.	Without the data then various coastline communities could eventually be affected.	When we updated our computer systems a few sections of the archive must have been missed, then years later nobody now knows what or where they are.

Statement about the issue:

❸ We have misplaced important meteorological data, needed for forecasting. We think it must have happened within the last fifty years when the archive system was updated. But the people who updated the archive record retired twenty years ago.

This tool is adapted from a blog by Tom Graves:
http://weblog.tetradian.com/2018/03/14/sensemaking-into-the-void/

How to define an organisation's vision
The Visioning tool

Photograph source: Flickr, Prince Roy. CGI Truck from Turbosquid

The scenario
In this imagined scenario a large logistics organisation based in Australia wants to explore their vision for *their* organisation. But they begin to realise they are just a small part in a much larger story *(or enterprise)*. So they use the **Visioning** tool to better understand everyone's vision and to see where their own vision fits into the larger story *(or enterprise)*.

About this tool
There are many tools available which help define an organisation's vision. This is typically framed as a definite goal such as: *The logistics firm wants to be the largest firm in Australia*. One problem with a having a specific goal can be; what happens if we reach that goal, what do we do then? The Tetradian **Visioning** tool works slightly differently by looking not just at the organisation's vision but the **overall** *(shared by all involved)* vision for the enterprise.
Knowing this can help people work together and not duplicate what others are doing.
Another advantage is that the tool allows you to treat the future in a more fluid way, rather than aiming for a specific point in the future. Therefore your organisation can regularly review its vision, as potentially a specific goal may not even be relevant anymore. The flip side of this can be to disrupt the overall vision, as there may be a better approach that no one has even considered. The **Visioning** tool asks you to examine the overall vision of all involved and then to see if what you want to do will support or disrupt that vision.

About this tool in brief
This version of the tool is used by an organisation to define what is the issue that affects an enterprise, what is done to address it and why it needs addressing. This will act as an anchor to check against all *their* strategic decisions.

To explore, resolve or address?
Throughout this book we talk about **exploring** or **resolving** issues, while this tool talks about **addressing** issues.
In this book we:
Explore an issue which may or may not need resolving or addressing.
Resolve an issue which has a definite end point.
Address an issue which has no definite end point, or needs constantly resolving.

Visioning tool

Mission identification:

All stakeholders vision for the enterprise

What is the overall issue that ***all*** stakeholders want to address?

What is done by the stakeholders to address the issue?

Why does the issue need addressing?

What value is generated by addressing the issue?

Our vision for the enterprise

What part of the overall issue do we want to address?

What do we want to do to address the issue?

Who will address the issue?

Does the issue have a specific finish point or is it ongoing?

What would we do next if the issue is resolved? (*Or didn't need resolving*).

What is our vision for the enterprise?
Key words which sum up our vision for our involvement in the enterprise.

Does our vision match with our Effectiveness criteria?
(*Use the **Effectiveness** tool on page 34 to cross-check*)

This tool is adapted from: Introduction to Visioning by Tom Graves
https://youtu.be/z0ybs2VOI-M

Where do you want to go?

How to use this tool

How can this tool help you?
This version of the tool is used to establish what is the issue which affects an overall enterprise, what is done to resolve it and why it needs resolving. This will then be used to create a meaningful vision statement, which will underpin everything your organisation does.

What needs to be done before using this tool?
In this example a mission is run to: *'Plan how to explore our vision for our organisation'.* Part of that mission would be to determine what they want the organisation to be. Some of that would be explored in the **Context folder**, where the **Visioning** tool would be used. The **Visioning** tool could be used with other context tools to set the context for the organisation which would then lead to the **Scope folder**. There they would explore options about how to actually achieve their vision.

How long would it take to complete a Visioning tool-sheet?
In this example a small team took about an hour to fill out the tool-sheet.

A brief guide to using the Visioning tool

❶ Note here the mission that the tool is being used for. For example to establish what the vision for the enterprise is.

❷ Here you look at the vision for the **overall** enterprise and explore who is doing what and why.

❸ Now you understand better the vision of the **overall** enterprise, here you explore what part **your** organisation will play in that enterprise. This can help confirm that your vision is relevant, or if maybe the vision itself could be challenged, such as disrupting the market with innovation.

❹ Here your vision statement is clarified in one short sentence and will act as the benchmark for your vision of the future.

❺ Here you use the **Effectiveness** tool *(See page 34)* connected to the **Visioning** tool to cross-check that your vision aligns with your choices for effectiveness.

What other tools work well with this tool?

Π The **Value** tool which can help define why something needs resolving by understanding its value. *(See page 6).*

Σ The **Sense making** tool can help define what the issue is that the organisation aims to resolve. *(See page 10).*

Φ The **Holomap** tool can be useful to better understand who an organisation's stakeholders are. *(See page 22).*

Ψ The **Where to start** tool can help to establish how to resolve an issue. *(See page 78).*

Visioning tool

Mission identification: Understand what the shared vision for our enterprise is.
Keep Australia supplied with equipment and supplies.

All stakeholders vision for the enterprise

What is the overall issue that **all** stakeholders want to address?
Keep Australia supplied with equipment and supplies so that Australia keeps functioning.

What is done by the stakeholders to address the issue?
We will use a Holomap tool to see who does what. Some examples include us, we have fifty trucks. The government keeps the roads maintained. Mines request supplies.

Why does the issue need addressing?   Look at Knock-on effects tool!
If companies such as mines don't keep supplied, they will be unable to function. This will have all kinds of negative knock-on effects such as loss of jobs and earnings.

What value is generated by addressing the issue?
We will use a Value tool to examine this. Some examples include financial, all the companies who supply the mines, communities, a national pride in working through adversity.

Our vision for the enterprise

What part of the overall issue do we want to address?
To supply the companies and communities, especially in Western Australia.

What do we want to do to address the issue?
We want to use our fleet of trucks to supply the companies and communities.

Who will address the issue?
We will use a Holomap tool to see who would do what. Some examples include our drivers, coordinators, mechanics, truck suppliers and fuel suppliers.

Does the issue have a specific finish point or is it ongoing?
It is on-going, there will always be a need to keep Australia supplied.

What would we do next if the issue is resolved? (*Or didn't need resolving*).
This type of issue we will continuously address, rather than resolve it with a set finish point.

What is our vision for the enterprise?
Key words which sum up our vision for our involvement in the enterprise.

Supply   Australia

Supplying Australia

Keeping Australia's businesses supplied.

Keeping Australia supplied.

Does our vision match with our Effectiveness criteria?
*(Use the **Effectiveness** tool on page 34 to cross-check)*
We feel that the vision does match with our Effectiveness criteria, which we set up before.

This tool is adapted from: Introduction to Visioning by Tom Graves
https://youtu.be/z0ybs2VOI-M

How to map an organisation's services
The Enterprise Canvas tool

Photograph source and CGI: Joseph Chittenden

The scenario
In this imagined scenario a Seychelles luxury hotel is proposing to fully automate their customer care system. But initial trials have shown problems dealing with more specialised complaints or requests.
Before deciding what to do next, the luxury hotel uses the **Enterprise Canvas tool** to map out the services currently offered and see what effect automation might potentially have on them.

About this tool in brief
This version of the tool is used as a visual checklist to understand what a service does, why it does it and what an organisation needs to effectively run that service.

About this tool
This is a simplified version of the **Enterprise Canvas** tool. The tool looks at what a service does, for example the Seychelles luxury hotel. In the central box we have:
The relationships and activities of the hotel, its suppliers and its customers. All of these combine to form a story of the hotel. The hotel is the organisation but it is not the enterprise, rather it is part of the enterprise.
The outer parts of the tool are ghosted to keep things less cluttered. These look at other external parts of the enterprise such as investors and beneficiaries. These parties will require value (*see the Value tool on page 6*) as will all parties involved. The upper part of the tool looks at how the organisation is run to best meet the needs of the service.
There is a more detailed book available which gives an in-depth look at what **Enterprise Canvas** is and what it is used for. See http://tetradianbooks.com/2010/11/ecanvas/

In brief
The **Enterprise Canvas** tool works well with the **Service Cycle** tool which breaks down the customer journey when using a service. *(See page 30).*

For information about how to use this tool see overleaf.

Enterprise Canvas tool

Mission identification:

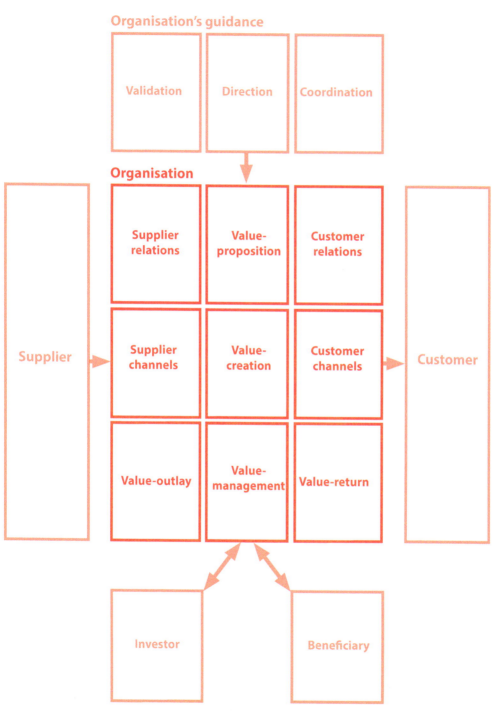

This tool is adapted from the Enterprise Canvas tool designed by Tom Graves
https://leanpub.com/tp-ecanvas

What are all the parts that make up a service?

How to use this tool

How can this tool help you?
This version of the tool is used to explore how you currently meet your customers' needs and other parties involved with the business story or enterprise.

What needs to be done before using this tool?
In this example the tool would most probably be used as part of a **Linked mission** (see Change-mapping book 1, page 36 and page 90 in this book).

How long would it take to complete an Enterprise Canvas tool-sheet?
In this example it took a few hours to complete the tool-sheet.

A brief guide to using the Enterprise Canvas tool

1. Note here the mission that the tool is being used for, such as to explore if automated customer care fits the hotel's needs.
2. Describe how your organisation finds suppliers and maintains their relationships with those suppliers.
3. Describe how your organisation will deliver value to all that are involved with the service, such as customers and suppliers.
4. Describe how your organisation finds customers and maintains their relationships with those customers.
5. Describe how suppliers connect with your organisation, such as local fishermen delivering fish to the hotel.
6. Describe how your organisation creates value. In our example hiring local tour guides rather than generic tours.
7. Describe how customers connect with your organisation, for example having friendly and approachable reception staff.
8. Describe how the supplier is paid by your organisation, such as making sure suppliers are paid on time, without delay.
9. Describe how your organisation manages consistent value, such as what profits do they have, does it all balance up?
10. Describe how your organisation is paid by the customer. In our example guests paying upon arrival.
11. Describe your organisation's suppliers and customers. In our example local food suppliers and French tourists.
12. Does your staff know and follow guidance. For example do they practice environmental sustainability?
13. Describe how management guides your organisation towards its vision, such as having clear leadership.
14. Describe how everything is coordinated within your organisation, such as good IT and regular staff meetings.
15. Describe the investors in your organisation, such as financial investment and investment from the local community.
16. Describe who are the beneficiaries in terms of value (see page 6) such as local businesses and families.

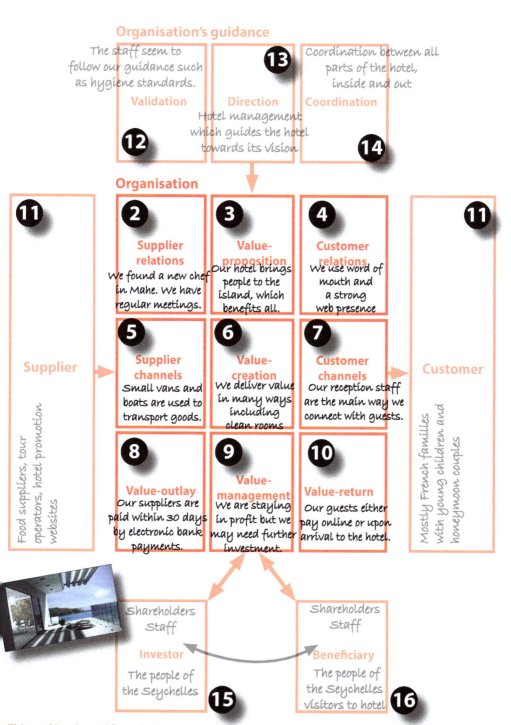

22. Big Picture scenarios

How to rationalise a supply chain
The Holomap tool

CGI Joseph Chittenden

About this tool in brief
This version of the tool is used to identify the stakeholders affected by an issue, and also identify what their relationships are with each other.

The scenario
In this imagined scenario an Australian wine producer is launching a new red wine.
The wine producer wants to rationalise their supply chain with an emphasis on sustainability. So they use the **Holomap** tool to map out all stakeholders involved with wine production either directly or indirectly.

About this tool
When trying to understand the causes of an issue or how to resolve an issue it can be useful to know who is involved.
This version of the **Holomap** tool is used to map out all the stakeholders involved with the issue. It does this by splitting the stakeholders into groups:
The first group sits in the *Transaction space*, which is where the suppliers, the organisation and clients are placed.
The next group sits in the *Market space*, these are individuals or parties who directly interact with the organisation such as competitors, regulators and journalists.
The next group is the *Shared Enterprise*, these are individuals or groups who indirectly interact with the organisation. These can be wide ranging and sometimes unexpected.
One of the categories here is *'world'* showing that sometimes a vast number can become involved in the enterprise, even if they didn't know they are.
The last group is *Investors and beneficiaries* who provide or receive value from the enterprise.

Holomap tool

Mission identification:

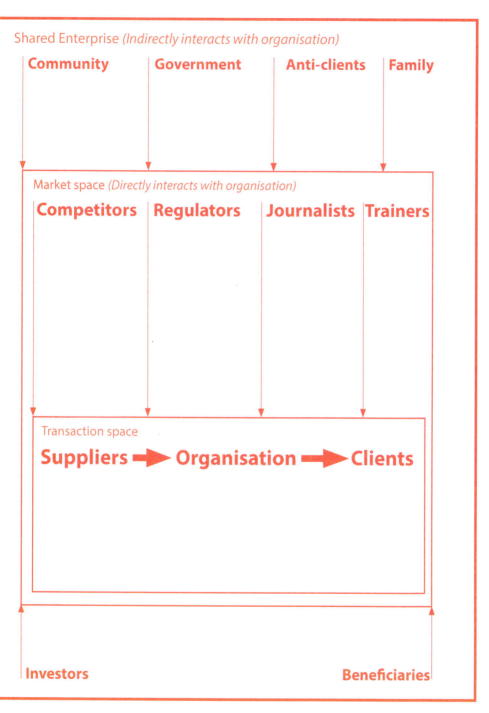

This tool is adapted from the *Holomap* tool designed by Tom Graves and Michael Smith.
http://weblog.tetradian.com/2014/09/18/organisation-and-enterprise/

Who are all the stakeholders in an organisation's story?

How to use this tool
How can this tool help you?
This version of the tool is used to map out who are the stakeholders within the context of the your issue. For example: Who are the suppliers? Who are other people indirectly involved such as regulators and government?

What needs to be done before using this tool?
In this example a mission is run to: 'Rationalise our supply chain, with an emphasis on sustainability'.
The **Holomap** tool is a **Context** folder tool. It is used to help understand the context of the issue, so that with the information found you can decide what you want to do next, rather than rushing to solve the wrong thing.

How long would it take to complete a Holomap tool-sheet?
In this example a small team took a couple of hours to sketch out the key stakeholders within the context. The information found would form the basis of future decision making.

A brief guide to using the Holomap tool
❶ Note here the mission that the tool is being used for. For example to rationalise the wine producer's supply chain.
❷ Note here who are the key stakeholders in the transaction space. In our example some might include timber post suppliers and customers based around the world.
❸ Note here who are the stakeholders in the market space who directly interact with your organisation. In our example: Other wine producers and wine journalists.
❹ Note here who are the stakeholders in shared enterprise *(all those who might be involved indirectly)*. In our example: Government departments and anti-clients *(anti-clients might be disgruntled customers or people who are opposed to the wine producer's environmental practices)*.
❺ Note here who are the investors who provide value *(These can be financial investors or communities investing trust and so on. See the **Value** tool on page 6 for more about types of value)*
Also note who are the beneficiaries who receive value.

What other tools work well with this tool?
Σ The **Visioning** tool can be used in combination with this tool to help identify what connects all these stakeholders together *(See page 14)*.
Π The **Inside/Out** tool can be useful here to better define how the organisation works internally and externally. *(See page 40)*.

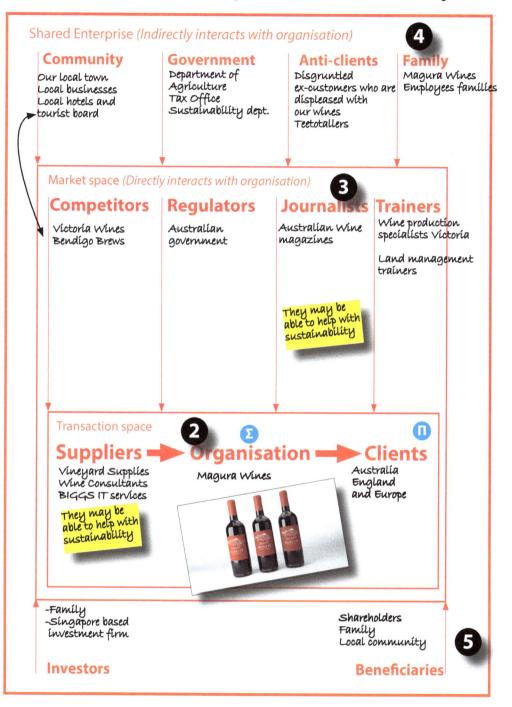

How to guide an organisation
The Guide tool

Photograph source: Flickr, Dan Nevill. CGI Truck from Turbosquid.

About this tool in brief
This version of the tool helps an organisation define what must stay constant and what can change when resolving an issue.

The scenario
A recently merged Australian logistics firm is looking at how they want to expand their services to cover the whole country. But they are unsure if this may take the firm away from their original vision. They decide to use the **Guide** tool to see if this new direction is the best way to proceed. Part of this is looking at what must stay constant and what can change.

About this tool
If we use our logistics firm as an example, they want to expand their reach across the whole of Australia. They can't decide whether to use a **Waterfall** or an **Agile** method. The **Waterfall** method uses a strict set of steps to manage projects, while **Agile** allows more experimentation and adaptability. Both have advantage and disadvantages. This version of the tool adds a backbone to combine **Waterfall** and **Agile**.
The later parts of the tool look at how these changes will be governed so that everyone is on the same page.
Also included is a MoSCoW tool *(designed by Dai Clegg)* which can help with defining what can change and what can't. This tool can be used to tackle individual issues or an enterprise. For an enterprise it would act as guidance about how to tackle any issue, when to rigidly follow guidelines and when to be more flexible. This can be particularly relevant in a rapidly changing situation. Another example is where an organisation rigidly sticks to what has worked in the past and refuses to change.

Guide tool

Mission identification:

What is the issue *(or enterprise)* we are resolving?

What part do we play in resolving the issue?

What items are unique to this organisation that allow us to resolve the issue?

What items are essential to our work and need to be shared across our organisation?

Define what must stay constant when resolving the issue. Using all of the items identified in the four previous steps. *(This is called the Backbone).*

The *MoSCoW* tool can help when filling out the question above.

Must have

Should have

Could have

Won't have (this time)

How will your team know what must stay constant *(Waterfall)* and what can be changed *(Agile)* when resolving the issue?

How will you keep control of what stays constant and what doesn't?

How will new items be added into the *'Backbone'* in the future?

This tool is adapted from:
weblog.tetradian.com/2011/06/17/architecting-the-enterprise-backbone/
www.slideshare.net/tetradian/vision-role-mission-goal-a-framework-for-business-motivation
MoSCoW method designed by Dai Clegg (Part 6 on this sheet)

Do you favour a step by step approach or do you like to leap into the future?

How to use this tool
How can this tool help you?
Agile is a method for managing projects using continuous testing rather than the **Waterfall** method where it follows a more rigid stage by stage approach. This tool combines the two methods by adding a **Backbone**. The **Backbone** allows the team to explore new ideas without losing sight of the overall goal.

What needs to be done before using this tool?
This tool is used in the **Context** folder, but is likely to be part of a set of scaled-up missions *(see page 106 in the first Change-mapping book)*. Preceding missions would have looked at why expanding their offer would be important to the firm, while in this mission the team are looking at how they will approach solving this and other issues. What is found here will act as a guide for how they explore or resolve any future issues.

How long would it take to complete a Guide tool-sheet?
In this example the logistics firm took a few hours to work through the sheet with detailed answers.

A brief guide to using the Guide tool
1 Note here the mission that the tool is being used for. For example to expand logistics services across Australia.

2 This section is used to define what the issue is. For example what the organisation does to resolve it and what they need to resolve the issue. All of these can be said to be part of the enterprise that the organisation is involved in.

3 This section uses the **MoSCoW method** *(Designed by Dai Clegg)* to refine what was found in the first section by asking what you must have to resolve the issue and other questions.

4 In this section we ask *'Where should the organisation favour an* **Agile** *or* **Waterfall** *method when tackling future issues?'* A mixture of this can add a **Backbone** to get the best of both worlds. Also how will the team know what can be changed and what can't?

What other tools work well with this tool?
Π The **Visioning** tool can be useful in defining what the vision of the organisation actually is. *(See page 14)*.

Σ The **Holomap** tool can be used to better define all the stakeholders and what the organisation's role is. *(See page 22)*.

Φ The **Knock-on effects** tool can show potential consequences of future changes to what can be changed and what can't. *(See page 68)*.

Guide tool

Mission identification: Expand our services to the whole of Australia.

What is the issue (or enterprise) we are resolving?

Our clients need regular supplies across the country, quickly and economically.

What part do we play in resolving the issue?

We deliver supplies to businesses across Australia.

What items are unique to this organisation that allow us to resolve the issue?

We have a large fleet of trucks and a team of logistics experts. We have over 40 years of experience in this area.

What items are essential to our work and need to be shared across our organisation?

Up to date communications between our team and our clients. Fully maintained fleet of 100 trucks. Real-time tracking.

Define what must stay constant when resolving the issue. Using all of the items identified in the four previous steps. *(This is called the Backbone)*.

Commitment to service, we get our clients supplies to their clients on time and on budget.

The *MoSCoW* tool can help when filling out the question above.

Must have Well maintained fleet of trucks and sufficient fuel. Location tracking.

Should have Good working conditions for our drivers, if they fail, we fail.

Could have Weather monitoring systems in the trucks.

Won't have (this time) Electric vehicles as this could be potentially difficult to use in the Outback.

How will your team know what must stay constant *(Waterfall)* and what can be changed *(Agile)* when resolving the issue?

Our planning guidelines will contain all our values, applicable standards which is made available to all staff members. This will be on our servers ready for staff to consult.

How will you keep control of what stays constant and what doesn't?

When we have new logistics projects we will tackle them case by case. Rather than a rigid approach to each case, we will stay 'in the spirit' of our guidelines. For example if new technology allows a more innovative solution, we would consider the benefits.

How will new items be added into the *'Backbone'* in the future?

We will have monthly reviews, if a new method or technology is seen as a benefit. But we need to have a long term testing procedure in case that a new method or technology has unexpected consequences.

This tool is adapted from:
weblog.tetradian.com/2011/06/17/architecting-the-enterprise-backbone/
www.slideshare.net/tetradian/vision-role-mission-goal-a-framework-for-business-motivation
MoSCoW method designed by Dai Clegg (Part 6 on this sheet)

How to see the customer's journey
The Service cycle tool

CGI Phone, Joseph Chittenden, CGI Pen Turbosquid

The scenario
In this imagined scenario an English bank wants to better understand their customer's journey when obtaining a bank loan. They use the **Service cycle** tool which looks at how the customer interacts with the bank through the different stages of acquiring a bank loan.

About this tool in brief
This tool looks at each stage of the customer journey from the view of the your customer and your organisation.

About this tool
This version of the tool looks at the customer journey when using a service.
The first section of the tool looks at how the customer finds out about the service and tentatively explores if the service fits with *their* story. As confidence in the organisation offering the service grows, the customer will move down the stages to eventually using the service. In our example the customer who wants a bank loan has come to the bank, prepared to obtain a loan and eventually has the loan.
The customer now having a loan means that the issue has been resolved. But as it is a service *cycle* then each of the previous stages will need to be reviewed.
So each stage is reviewed, for example how was the process of obtaining the actual loan achieved. Is there room for improvement if another potential customer wanted a loan. These lessons tend to have knock-on effects, up and down the service cycle.
At the end of using this tool you should be able to see where a service can be improved from its initial design through to its everyday use.

In brief
Some organisations try to short-cut some of these stages. While this can seem to be more profitable in the short-term, in the long term things can collapse without warning, because relations and reputations are not properly maintained.

Service cycle tool
Mission identification:

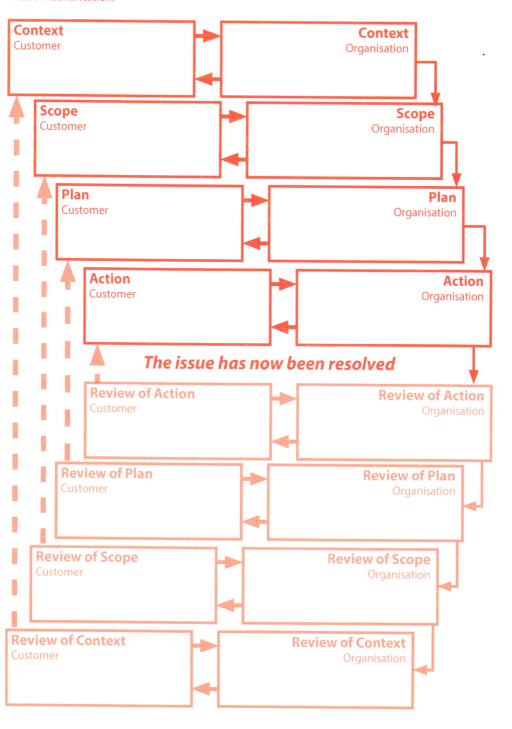

This tool is adapted from a blog by Tom Graves.
http://weblog.tetradian.com/2015/04/13/rbpea-basics-and-fundamentals/

Understanding the customer is the best way to help them.

How to use this tool

How can this tool help you?
This version of the tool is used to explore distinct phases of a customer's journey from the point of view of the customer and the organisation.

What needs to be done before using this tool?
In this example a mission is run to: *'Explore how the customer currently obtains one of our bank loans'.* This would be explored in the **Context folder**, where this tool is used. This Context mission would likely be part of a larger set of linked missions looking at the bank's overall strategy. *(See page 108 in the first Change-mapping book for more about large scale missions.)*

How long would it take to complete a Service cycle tool-sheet?
In this example the bank, working with trusted customers, took a few hours to complete the tool.

A brief guide to using the Service cycle tool

❶ Note here the mission that the tool is being used for. For example to see how a customer obtains a bank loan.

❷ This part of the tool looks at the customer journey from where the customer is tentatively exploring the service down to the actual usage of the service. This is broken down into four stages. In addition the journey is also viewed from the organisation's point of view.

❸ In this part the service has been used or the issue has been resolved, so in our example the customer now has a bank loan.

❹ In this part each stage of the customer journey is reviewed. This can highlight problem areas, for example although most of the customer journey was problem free, the **Plan** stage had a few problems.

Another useful feature of this tool is the ability to see the difference between what the customer sees and what the organisation sees.

What other tools work well with this tool?

Π The **Visioning** tool can be useful defining what the vision of the organisation actually is. *(See page 14).*

Σ The **Inside Out** tool can be used to further define how the organisation functions internally and externally. *(See page 40).*

Φ The **SEMPER** tool helps identify disparities between different parties at each stage of the cycle. *(See page 60).*

Ψ The **SCAN** tool can show uncertainties to do with time and complexity, when trying to resolve the bank loan. *(See page 82).*

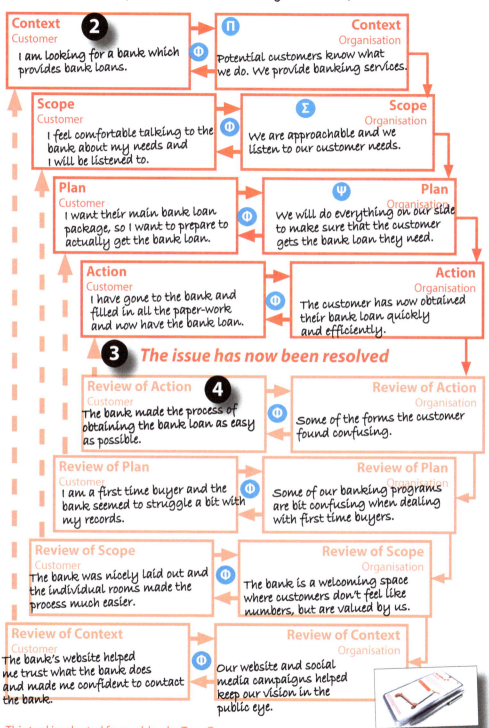

How to be effective
The Effectiveness tool

Photograph source: CGTextures. CGI Drone, Joseph Chittenden

About this tool in brief
This tool acts as guidance across the organisation and is referred to when resolving issues or as part of the enterprise.

The scenario
In this imagined scenario, a British drone manufacturer has noticed that certain projects work well in isolation, but don't fit well with the overall organisation. They decide to create a set of simple guidelines which will be referred to by all in the organisation, when working on any project.

About this tool
This version of the tool is used to create guidance across an organisation. This would be used from small scale tasks up to how the whole organisation functions.

The tool looks at five key areas to see how the organisation currently functions. A small team would then fill in each part of the tool, for example: *'How integrated is the organisation?'* The main point of this tool is not to give a strict set of rules for a set project, but rather a set of general guidelines which can be used by *anyone* doing *anything* within the organisation. For example in the **Appropriate** section this would look at what fits with the organisation's vision. If we said our drone manufacturer wants to use more sustainable methods, then this would range from improved water usage during manufacturing down to printing fewer emails.

Another point to note is that each part of the tool connects to the other, so the sustainable production methods which are *'appropriate'* would be also be more *'efficient'*, for example. The information found here can be used with other tools such as the **Score** tool *(see page 74)*.

Effectiveness tool

Mission identification:

Efficient
When resolving the issue: skills, equipment, etc are used as efficiently as possible.

Reliable
When resolving the issue we use predictable and consistent methods.

Integrated
When resolving the issue, all the organisation is coordinated and shares information to all that need it.

Elegant
When resolving the issue, what to do is clear, consistent and simple to understand for all involved.

Appropriate
Resolving the issue fits with our vision for the organisation.

This tool is adapted from a blog written by Tom Graves.
http://weblog.tetradian.com/2016/08/28/on-effectiveness-solutions-story/

How can an organisation be more effective in all they do?

How to use this tool

How can this tool help you?
This version of the tool is used to establish effectiveness guidelines which can be used throughout the organisation.

What needs to be done before using this tool?
In this example a mission is run to: *'Create guidance for use across the whole drone manufacturing firm*. This would be explored in the **Context folder**, where this tool is used. This Context mission would likely be part of a larger set of linked missions looking at the drone manufacturer's overall strategy. *(See page 108 in the first Change-mapping book for more about large scale missions.)*

How long would it take to complete an Effectiveness tool-sheet?
In this example the drone manufacturer took a few hours to explore how these guidelines would affect the whole company.

A brief guide to using the Effectiveness tool

❶ Note here the mission that the tool is being used for, such as to create guidance for the drone manufacturing firm.

❷ Here efficiency guidelines are explored, which can be used across the whole organisation. Such as reducing waste and energy use.

❸ Here reliability guidelines are explored, which can be used across the entire organisation. An example might be using predictable and reliable IT systems.

❹ Here integration guidelines are explored, which can be used across the organisation. This might using work management programs to track teams' progress.

❺ Here guidelines are explored, which can be used across the organisation to make everything for all involved as simple as possible. For example all using metric measurements, rather than some using metric measurements and some using imperial measurements.

❻ Here guidelines are explored, which can be used across the organisation to make sure that all work done supports the organisation's vision.

What other tools work well with this tool?

Π The **Sense-making** tool can confirm that what is said to be *'simple and self-evident'* really is. *(See page 10).*

Σ The **Visioning** tool can be useful in defining what the vision of the organisation actually is. *(See page 14).*

Φ The **Guide** tool can be used in combination with this tool looking at what can be changed and what can't when resolving issues. *(See page 26).*

Effectiveness tool

Mission identification: Create guidance for use across the whole drone manufacturing firm.

Efficient
When resolving the issue: skills, equipment, etc are used as efficiently as possible.

All projects will follow our standard proven procedures to reduce waste. For example improving waste metal recovery in the machine shop.

Reliable
When resolving the issue we use predictable and consistent methods.

We will create guidelines based on what has worked before and what we believe will work in the future.
For example use After Action Reviews to support continuous improvement.

Integrated
When resolving the issue, all the organisation is coordinated and shares information to all that need it.

All projects will have 'project champions' who will coordinate between management and work-teams to make sure that the staff have all they need to complete the project. While keeping management aware of the project status.

All projects will follow our standard approaches unless information shows a better approach. Work instructions are clear and simple to follow.

All projects will support our commitment to safety and innovation. For example that safety procedures are understood and followed.

Elegant
When resolving the issue, what to do is clear, consistent and simple to understand for all involved.

Appropriate
Resolving the issue fits with our vision for the organisation.

This tool is adapted from a blog written by Tom Graves.
http://weblog.tetradian.com/2016/08/28/on-effectiveness-solutions-story/

Chapter 2: People issues scenarios
Scope folder tools in action

NOTE
All the scenarios are hypothetical and fiction. The organisations mentioned are used to illustrate a specific issue to better describe how the tools could be used.

Downloadable tools
Available at the time of writing to download are PDFs and PowerPoint slides of the tools shown in this chapter.
https://www.changemappingbook.com/scope-tools

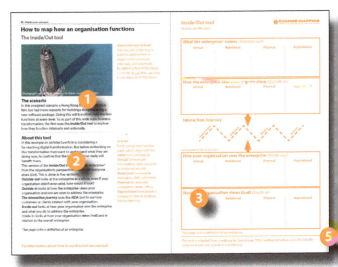

About these tools
In this chapter we look at tools used to explore the people issues affecting how an issue or enterprise is resolved.
In the first *Change-mapping* book a simple **Scope** tool was used, here we look at eight new **Scope** tools.
The tools in this chapter are used to:
- Map how an organisation functions inside and out.
- Establish strategies for resolving rapidly changing issues.
- Define leadership requirements.
- Establish strategies for building skilled teams.
- Establish strategies for balanced teams.
- Find out what really is happening within an organisation.
- Find out the story of an organisation.
- Prepare for unexpected knock-on effects.

The scenarios
In order to show how these new **Scope** tools work, we have created eight scenarios. Each scenario has a real world issue which uses one of the tools to explore, address or resolve the issue.
It is important to note that any of the tools could be used in any scenario and are not limited to only being used within that specific scenario.

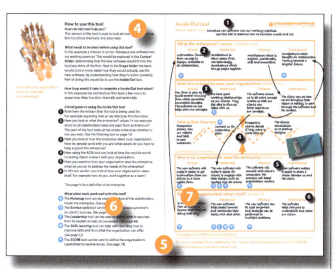

How to use this chapter
How can these tools help you?
These tools are used to explore the people issues within an issue or enterprise. This will be vital when resolving issues by fully understanding the *'who'* of an issue.

What needs to be done before using these tools?
You should read the first *Change-mapping* book, as this will show you how everything works and how to add more detailed tools, such as the ones shown in this chapter.

A brief guide to using this chapter
Each tool is discussed over four pages

- A scenario showing the *Change-mapping* tool in use exploring a real world issue.
- A general description of the tool discussing when and what it is used for.
- A blank version of the tool which can be copied and used in your own *Change-mapping* missions.
- Instructions showing how to use each tool including what needs to be done *before* using the tool.
- A link to where you can find out more information about the tool online.
- A list of other tools in the book which work well with the tool shown.
- A filled-in example of the tool which uses the scenario to help you understand how to use the tool.

Using these tools in a Change-mapping mission

1. Set up a mission to explore or resolve an issue, with a **Mission start folder**.

2. Use a **Context folder** to explore the context of the issue.

2. Use a **Scope folder** to explore the people issues. If the basic Scope folder doesn't generate enough information add one of the tools from this chapter, which best fit your requirements.

3. If the tool generates enough information then move to the **Plan folder**.

How to map how an organisation functions
The Inside/Out tool

Photograph source: Flickr, Jacopo, CGI Tower, Joseph Chittenden

About this tool in brief
This version of the tool is used to explore how an organisation functions internally and externally. By defining how it functions currently, it can then see how it can improve in the future.

The scenario
In this imagined scenario a Hong Kong based architecture firm has had more requests for buildings designed using a new software package. Doing this will transform how the firm functions at every level. So as part of this wide scale business transformation, the firm uses the **Inside/Out tool** to explore how they function internally and externally.

About this tool
In this example an architecture firm is considering a far-reaching digital transformation. But before embarking on this transformation they want to understand what they are doing now, to confirm that the transformation really will benefit them.

This version of the **Inside/Out** tool looks at an enterprise from the organisation's perspective *(Inside)* and everyone else's *(Out)*. This is done in five sections:

Outside-out looks at the enterprise as a whole, even if your organisation didn't even exist, how would it look?
Outside-in looks at how the enterprise views your organisation and you are seen to address the enterprise.
The interaction journey uses the AIDA tool to see how customers or clients interact with your organisation.
Inside-out looks at how your organisation sees the enterprise and what you do to address the enterprise.
Inside-in looks at how your organisation views itself and in relation to the overall enterprise.

In brief
Each orange box has four parts which align with the *Value* tool *(see page 6)*:
Virtual for example information, data, accounts or historical records.
Relational for example managers, staff, customers.
Physical for example computers, desks, offices.
Aspirational for example a company's brand, strategy, future planning.

Inside/Out tool

Mission identification:

What the enterprise values *(Outside-out)*

Virtual	Relational	Physical	Aspirational

How the enterprise sees your organisation *(Outside-in)*

Virtual	Relational	Physical	Aspirational

Interaction Journey

Awareness — Interest — Desire — Action

AIDA designed by Elias St. Elmo Lewis.

How your organisation sees the enterprise *(Inside-out)*

Virtual	Relational	Physical	Aspirational

How your organisation views itself *(Inside-in)*

Virtual	Relational	Physical	Aspirational

This tool is adapted from a weblog by Tom Graves *http://weblog.tetradian.com/2012/06/06/inside-in-inside-out-outside-in-outside-out/*

How does your organisation function internally and externally?

How to use this tool

How can this tool help you?
This version of the tool is used to look at how the architecture firm functions internally and externally.

What needs to be done before using this tool?
In this example a mission is run to: *'Introduce new software into our working practices'.* This would be explored in the **Context** folder, determining that the new software would fit into the business story of the firm. Next in the **Scope** folder the team would look in more detail how they would actually use the new software, by understanding how they function currently. Part of doing this would be to use the **Inside/Out** tool.

How long would it take to complete a Inside/Out tool-sheet?
In this example the architecture firm took a few hours to assess how they function internally and externally.

A brief guide to using the Inside/Out tool

❶ Note here the mission that the tool is being used for. For example exploring how an architecture firm functions.

❷ Here you look at what the enterprise values. In our example what do all stakeholders need and want from architecture? This part of the tool looks at the whole enterprise whether or not you exist. *(See the Visioning tool on page 14)*

❸ Here you look at how the enterprise views your organisation. How do people work with you and what assets do you have to help support the enterprise?

❹ Here using the AIDA tool you look at how the outside world including clients interact with your organisation.

❺ Here you examine how your organisation sees the enterprise, what do you do to address the needs of the enterprise?

❻ In this last section you look at how your organisation views itself. For example how do you work together as a team?

What other tools work well with this tool?

Θ The **Holomap** tool can be used to explore all the stakeholders, inside the enterprise. *(See page 22).*

Π The **Service cycle** tool can be used to explore a customer's (or client's) journey. *(See page 30).*

Σ The **Leadership** tool can be used to define what is required from its leaders to help all concerned. *(See page 48).*

Φ The **Skills learning** tool can help with deciding how to improve skills and thus what the organisation can offer. *(See page 52).*

Ψ The **SCORE** tool can be used to define the organisation's capabilities to resolve issues. *(See page 74).*

Inside/Out tool

Mission identification: Introduce new software into our working practices.
Use this tool to examine how we function inside and out.

What the enterprise values *(Outside-out)*

Virtual	Relational	Physical	Aspirational
Information flowing from concept to design, available to all stakeholders.	Architecture is about people first, not technology. Architecture which brings people together.	Architecture which is: elegant, sustainable, safe and innovative.	Architecture which benefits all stakeholders. Moving towards a brighter future.
Θ		Θ	

How the enterprise sees your organisation *(Outside-in)*

Virtual	Relational	Physical	Aspirational
Our firm is seen as a multi-award winning firm which generates innovative concepts. The software we use helps show our concepts.	We have good working relationships we our clients. They feel able to discuss ideas with us.	The software allows us to 3D print concept models so that our clients can better experience our concepts.	The client can see how we are bringing their vision to reality, in part through the software and its renders.
Π			

Interaction Journey Π

Prospective clients view our website and talk to past customers. — *Awareness*

Contact us for credentials pitch. — *Interest*

Prospective clients decide if they want to work with us. — *Desire*

The clients commission us to produce designs. — *Action*

AIDA designed by Elias St. Elmo Lewis.

How your organisation sees the enterprise *(Inside-out)*

Virtual	Relational	Physical	Aspirational
The new software will make it easier to get information from our clients in a more usable form.	The new software will make it easier for clients to engage with their design such as renders and 3D prints.	The software will connect with client's computers. For example web based presentation renders.	New software makes it easier to share a vision between us and the client.
Ψ	Π Φ Ψ	Ψ	

How your organisation views itself *(Inside-in)*

Virtual	Relational	Physical	Aspirational
A clear information flow so everyone knows what they are doing and why.	The new software helps people connect and coordinate their tasks with each other.	The new software can be used anywhere and backups can be performed in multiple locations.	The software helps everyone to understand and share our vision.
		Ψ	

This tool is adapted from a weblog by Tom Graves http://weblog.tetradian.com/2012/06/06/inside-in-inside-out-outside-in-outside-out/

How to resolve rapidly changing issues
The Decision tool

Photograph source: Flickr-Deensel.

About this tool in brief
This version of the tool is used to explore how an organisation makes individual decisions and groups of decisions.

The scenario
In this imagined scenario the Buenos Aires transport department want to trial two new tram lines between the airport and the city centre. They model different scenarios of tram use to see how the trams could work.
Part of this exercise includes using the **Decision** tool to see what might be the best options for trams and the city.

About this tool
This version of the tool breaks down the process of individual and group decisions within an organisation.
The decision making process is broken down into **Sense, Make Sense, Decide** and **Act**. This tool develops on the OODA loop designed by USAF Colonel John Boyd.
Part of the tool looks in more detail about how the decisions are made within the organisation. Sometimes decisions can be made without really understanding how one came to choose that decision.
The rest of the tool looks at how groups of decisions are made. While individual decisions can solve a single issue, sometimes groups of individual decisions can be at odds with each other. By noting each favourable outcome next to each other, we can see potential compromises which will solve the collective groups of issues rather than just the one.
This tool has been inspired by decision making seen in swarms, shoals and flocks in nature. It has been shown that individual creatures are likely to be picked off by predators. But by making decisions collectively and communicating in real time, small creatures can join into formidable groups.

Decision tool

Mission identification:

Task to be resolved (How would the issue be resolved)

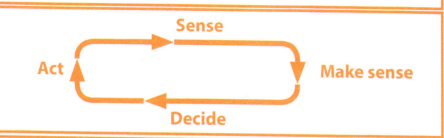

How are decisions made in the organisation?
https://en.wikipedia.org/wiki/Decision-making#Decision-making_techniques

Task to be resolved (How will the group of decisions be made to suit all stakeholders)

Note individual best decision outcome ⟶
Note collective best decision outcome --→

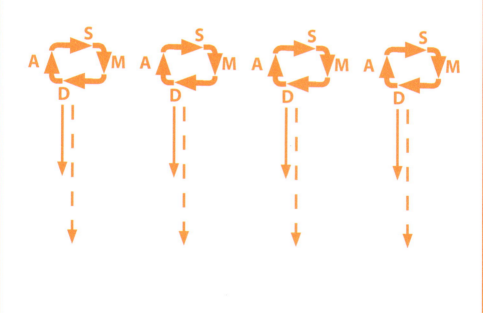

This tool is adapted from a weblog written by Tom Graves.
http://weblog.tetradian.com/2018/04/11/sensemaking-and-the-flocking-of-boyds/

By working together an organisation can overcome large issues.

How to use this tool

How can this tool help you?
This version of the tool is used to explore how an organisation makes individual decisions and groups of decisions.

What needs to be done before using this tool?
Set-up a mission to explore an issue, this is a **Scope** folder tool, so you will need to know the Context first, using the **Context** folder and a Mission Start folder.

How long would it take to complete a Decision tool-sheet?
If a team is looking at individual decisions then about an hour, if groups of decisions are being investigated then up to a day.

A brief guide to using the Decision tool

❶ Note here the mission that the tool is being used for. For example exploring an organisation's decision making.

❷ In this part you state the task to be resolved, which may differ from an overall mission's objectives.

❸ In this part you break down what makes up the parts of the decision making process.

❹ This part of the tool asks you for more detail about how decisions are made currently and has a link to more information about decision making techniques.

❺ This part of the tool looks at how groups of decisions can affect each other. Each SMDA loop can have its own decision *(shown with the orange lines)* but these may not favour all involved. The dashed orange lines represent decisions which favour the overall group. For example four sets of trams need to get to an airport at about the same time. The solid orange lines show that each tram can get to the airport, but will clash with other trams so none get through. By looking at the overall goal then a different result is required, in this case combining trams into a dedicated airport service and slightly shifting the other trams. This way all can get to the airport. In our example we have four groups of decisions, but many more could be catered for if required.

What other tools work well with this tool?

Π The **Sense-making** tool can be useful when exploring the context. *(See page 10).*

Σ The **Leadership** tool can be useful for help with decision making approaches. *(See page 48).*

Φ The **Knock-on effects** tool can be useful to look at unexpected consequences. *(See page 68).*

Decision tool

Mission identification: Link our tram system with the airport flights to improve tourism

Task to be resolved *(How would the issue be resolved)*
Improve tram connections from airport to centre of Buenos Aires.

Sense — Flight 001 should land at Buenos Aires international airport around 8.30

Make sense — Confirm that Flight 001 lands at 08.32 at Buenos Aires International airport

Decide — Have tram BA97 ready to meet plane for 08.32

Act — Tram BA97 leaves depot ready to meet flight 001 : 08.32

How are decisions made in the organisation?
https://en.wikipedia.org/wiki/Decision-making#Decision-making_techniques

We present our ideas to the team and make a group decision, if no one can decide we use the leader for the final decision.

Task to be resolved *(How will the group of decisions be made to suit all stakeholders)*
Improve tram connections from airport to centre of Buenos Aires for flights from four different countries arriving at same time, but with only two tram tracks.

Note individual best decision outcome →
Note collective best decision outcome ⇢

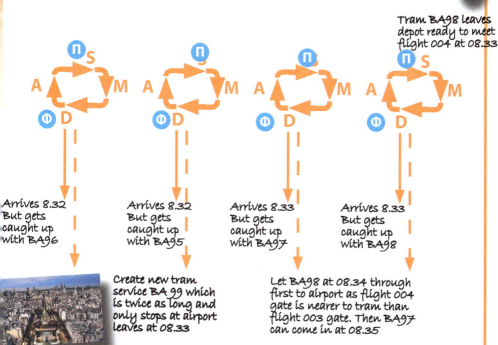

Tram BA98 leaves depot ready to meet flight 004 at 08.33

Arrives 8.32 But gets caught up with BA96

Arrives 8.32 But gets caught up with BA95 → Create new tram service BA 99 which is twice as long and only stops at airport leaves at 08.33

Arrives 8.33 But gets caught up with BA97

Arrives 8.33 But gets caught up with BA98 → Let BA98 at 08.34 through first to airport as flight 004 gate is nearer to tram than flight 003 gate. Then BA97 can come in at 08.35

This tool is adapted from a weblog written by Tom Graves.
http://weblog.tetradian.com/2018/04/11/sensemaking-and-the-flocking-of-boyds/

48. People issues scenarios

How to define leadership requirements
The Leadership tool

Photograph source: Wikipedia, USDA, Deerfire

About this tool in brief
This version of the tool is used to assess the qualities required for an organisation's leaders.

The scenario
In this scenario we can imagine that a California based server farm has concerns about the impacts of wildfires on their business. They want to explore how their staff would cope under difficult conditions, so they use the **Leadership** tool. This poses a set of questions about how a leader would resolve an issue, such as creating a disaster recovery plan.

About this tool
Asking a leader if they feel they are a good leader is likely to result in them saying *'Yes I am!'*. A more useful exercise would be to **see** if they are. The **Leadership** tool does this by asking the leader to show how they would deal with a scenario with multiple problems. How they answer each question should show their thought processes under difficult conditions. Although asking a leader *'How good a leader are you?'* could be politically tricky, there would be benefits in seeing how they and their team would function as a unit.

Sometimes high-level management can seem to lack connection to front-line tasks. In this situation a *'storm on the horizon'* would likely be highlighted by the **SEMPER** tool *(see page 60)*. The results of that tool would often show the disparity between staff and management. Logically then the leadership would be explored as well as the staff, which is where the **Leadership** tool could help.

We need leaders to guide the process of change, at every scale, from the smallest *(a single step in a business-process)* to the largest *(the purpose and strategy of the enterprise as a whole)*.

In brief
Using this tool-sheet the leader would give answers about how they would respond, in a certain scenario It can be useful to do tests or simulations to see what actually happens in that scenario.
Afterwards use an after action tool such as the one shown on page 94 of the first Change-mapping book, to assess how to improve performance and what the leader can improve.

Leadership tool

Mission identification:

Task to resolve an issue

Testing leadership qualities *What would the leader do under these conditions?*

Context questions
How would you establish the big-picture which surrounds the issue?
How would you establish vision, values, regulations and more while resolving the issue?
How would you establish success criteria while resolving the issue?

Scope questions
How would you establish who are the stakeholders affected by the issue?
How would you establish the scope of a project to resolve the issue?
How would you establish the requirements of a project to resolve the issue?
How would you establish the priorities of a project to resolve the issue?
How would you establish the skills required to resolve uncertainties?
How would you resolve clashes between stakeholders and staff?

Plan questions
How would you plan to resolve the task, step by step?
How would you create communication between departments, while resolving the task?
How would you create coordination between departments, while resolving the task?
How would you resolve the task with a reduced budget, and no access to more funds?
How would you resolve the task with reduced staff, and no more were available?
How would you resolve the task with reduced information, and none was available?
How would you resolve the task with reduced equipment, and no more was available?
How would you resolve the task with reduced time, and no more was available?
How would you resolve the task with less space, and no more was available?

Action questions
How would you tackle staff panic while trying to resolve the task?
How would you record the task being resolved, for future reference?

Review questions
How would you compare the task's resolution against the success criteria?
How would you support quality, skills and process improvement?
What would you do differently if the task was repeated?

This tool is adapted from a weblog written by Tom Graves.
http://weblog.tetradian.com/2016/06/10/managers-and-leaders/

Can a leader really do what they claim they can?

How to use this tool

How can this tool help you?
This tool assesses how you would resolve a task under different conditions. This will give information about how you are working currently and what could be improved.

What needs to be done before using this tool?
This is typically used as a **Scope** folder tool which looks at options to resolve issues as well as people issues. A **Scope** folder is used after a **Mission Start** folder and **Context** folder has been set up to explore or resolve an issue.

How long would it take to complete a Leadership tool-sheet?
This tool would most probably take a couple of hours answering the questions and then looking at what can be improved regarding leadership.

A brief guide to using the Leadership tool

❶ Note here the mission that the tool is being used for. For example to assess leadership candidates.

❷ Here you add a task which the person answering the questions will have to resolve.

❸ Here the person filling out the tool-sheet will be posed a set of questions. Each of the questions could stop the issue being resolved. How they are answered would show how that person approaches problem solving.

The questions are split into five categories which align with how *Change-mapping* works, such as Context questions, Scope questions and so on.

The questions, of course, can not cover every possible eventuality, but do cover some of the most important areas to consider. As with some of the other tools in this book, it gets conversations started, and extra questions could be added to provide further detail.

What other tools work well with this tool?

- Θ The **Sense-making** tool can be useful when exploring the context of an issue. *(See page 10)*.
- Λ The **Visioning** tool can be used to define what an organisation's vision is. *(See page 14)*.
- Ξ The **Modes** tool can be used to assess what qualities would be needed when assembling a team. *(See page 56)*.
- Σ The **Knock-on effects** tool can be useful to look at unexpected consequences of actions. *(See page 68)*.
- Φ The **Where to start** tool can be useful when exploring how to resolve an issue *(See page 78)*.
- Ψ The **SCAN** tool can be useful when planning how to resolve issues with unknown time and complexity. *(See page 82)*.

Leadership tool

Mission identification: Test how leadership candidates deal with different issues.

Task to resolve an issue
Create a disaster recovery plan to cope with increasing California wildfires.

Testing leadership qualities *What would the leader do under these conditions?*

Context questions
How would you establish the big-picture which surrounds the issue?
Establish the context, understand the issue, why is it important, who is involved. Page 68 Book 1**.
How would you establish vision, values, regulations and more while resolving the issue?
What is the server farm's vision, what do they value and local gov regs. Page 68 Book 1**.
How would you establish success criteria while resolving the issue?
Examine the context and talk to management and staff. Page 68 Book 1**.

Scope questions
How would you establish who are the stakeholders affected by the issue?
I would use the Holomap tool to look at stakeholders and their relationships.
How would you establish the scope of a project to resolve the issue?
Look at what is realistic to achieve with time and budget allowance. Page 78 Book 1**.
How would you establish the requirements of a project to resolve the issue?
See if there are older disaster recovery plans, what can be learnt as well.
How would you establish the priorities of a project to resolve the issue?
Look at running a small scale simulated disaster to see how we would react and gain insights.
How would you establish the skills required to resolve uncertainties?
Run a small scale simulated disaster to see how we would react and gain insights and information.
How would you resolve clashes between stakeholders and staff?
Try to understand the causes of the clashes and remove them.

Plan questions
How would you plan to resolve the task, step by step?
Run simulation (small scale) where wildfire is 5 miles away, what skills, equipment, etc do we need?
How would you create communication between departments, while resolving the task?
In simulation see what communication we need to be effective.
How would you create coordination between departments, while resolving the task?
Possibly have a disaster recovery team leader who would regularly train.
How would you resolve the task with a reduced budget, and no access to more funds?
Look at what has to be saved and what does not. People, then the servers.
How would you resolve the task with reduced staff, and no more were available?
Linked to last question. Save people and then as much as is safe to remove such as the servers.
How would you resolve the task with reduced information, and none was available?
Create better information channels! Situation can change rapidly.
How would you resolve the task with reduced equipment, and no more was available?
Before wildfire, warn that server farm can't be saved with reduced equipment.
How would you resolve the task with reduced time, and no more was available?
Simulation should give insights about this.
How would you resolve the task with less space, and no more was available?
Again the simulation should give insights about this.

Action questions
How would you tackle staff panic while trying to resolve the task?
Simulation should make people familiar with situation and less likely to panic.
How would you record the task being resolved, for future reference?
Video the simulation and then all watch it afterwards.

Review questions
How would you compare the task's resolution against the success criteria?
Ultimately if we encounter a wildfire and plan works as hoped.
How would you support quality, skills and process improvement?
More simulations, get in experts and more training.
What would you do differently if the task was repeated?
I think the simulation would show what could be done better.

** Book 1=The first Change-mapping book.
This tool is adapted from a weblog written by Tom Graves.
http://weblog.tetradian.com/2016/06/10/managers-and-leaders/

How to build a skilled team
The Skills Learning tool

CGI e-scooter, Joseph Chittenden

About this tool in brief
This version of the tool is used to provide support and guidance for the individual and the organisation during skills learning.

The scenario
In this imagined scenario a Stockholm, Sweden based manufacturing company has lost a number of key design staff to other companies. They now face a skills shortage. They use the **Skills Learning** tool to explore how they currently acquire skills and ways which can improve that process.

About this tool
Learning new skills would seem to be a linear process, in that you learn the skill and progressively improve.
But in practice learning a new skill matches more of the backwards and forwards progression as shown in the diagram on the right. The learner is aiming for perfection which being pragmatic can never be achieved. As the learner progresses from beginner, often mistakes will be made with the learner feeling that they can't ever master the new skill.
Eventually through trial and error the person will become highly proficient, but even then unexpected things can happen. So this version of the **Skills learning** tool has been designed to accommodate this non-linear skills learning process.
It does this by helping the learner measure where they feel they are in the skills learning journey and where the organisation can help them progress further.
So at key stages the learner will fill out a quick interview to see where the organisation can offer more value.
These values match the **Value** tool (*see page 6*) and represent better information, better hardware or experts to give advice. All of this should making learning new skills less daunting and more of a team effort.

In brief
Some examples of the types of things found in the table (below right).
Virtual: *video tutorials.*
Relational: *Industry experts, colleagues who have skills which they can teach.*
Physical: *Computers, tools, programs, etc to make the staff members job easier.*
Aspirational: *Helping staff members reach their goals in life, rather than staff feeling like cogs in a machine.*

Skills learning tool

Mission identification:

What stage are you at learning your new skill?

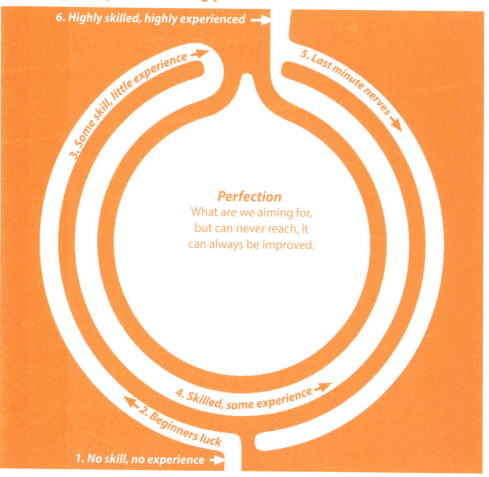

Rate how your organisation supports skills learning.

Virtual	Relational	Physical	Aspirational

This tool is adapted from the Skills Labyrinth tool designed by Tom Graves.
http://weblog.tetradian.com/2015/08/19/seven-sins-7-lost-in-the-learning-labyrinth/

The path to learning skills is not always the most direct one.

How to use this tool
How can this tool help you?
This version of the tool is used to assess how you feel your skills learning is progressing and how your organisation can improve that process.

What needs to be done before using this tool?
In this example a mission is run to: *'Plan how to improve skills acquisition'.* Part of that mission would be to see if skills are being acquired. Some of that would be explored in the **Context** folder. This tool would be used in the **Scope** folder to help orient the company towards the most effective way to improve skills learning.

How long would it take to complete a Skills Learning tool-sheet?
In this example the designer would use the tool every month to review their own progress and the company's towards skills learning with each review taking a few minutes.

A brief guide to using the Skills learning tool

❶ Note here the mission that the tool is being used for. For example exploring how a staff member is acquiring new skills for their work.

❷ You use this section to mark where you feel you are in the skills learning process. This is reviewed each month, to rate progress and skill retention.

❸ Here you rate how your organisation supports skills learning. You give each box a mark out of five.
  1. Your organisation does not support skills learning.
  2. Your organisation supports skills learning with limited information, experts, equipment and staff goals.
  3. Your organisation supports skills learning with some information, experts, equipment and staff goals.
  4. Your organisation supports skills learning with plenty of information, experts, equipment and staff goals.
  5. Your organisation supports skills learning with large amounts of information, experts, equipment and staff goals.

What other tools work well with this tool?
Π The **Value** tool uses the same *'value'* categories to define what skills are valued and why. *(See page 6).*
Σ The **Visioning** tool can be useful in cross-checking that the skills are acquired are useful to the organisation. *(See page 14).*
Φ The **Inside/Out** tool can also be used to confirm that skills learnt align with what the organisation requires. *(See page 40).*
Ψ The **SEMPER** tool can help give the staff member a voice, if they feel that they need help to obtain skills. *(See page 60).*

Skills learning tool

Mission identification: How do we learn new visualising skills in our manufacturing company

What stage are you at learning your new skill?

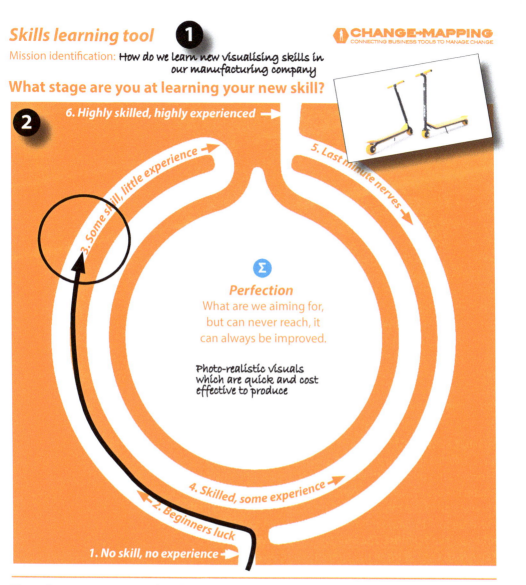

- 1. No skill, no experience
- 2. Beginners luck
- 3. Some skill, little experience
- 4. Skilled, some experience
- 5. Last minute nerves
- 6. Highly skilled, highly experienced

Perfection
What are we aiming for, but can never reach, it can always be improved.

Photo-realistic visuals which are quick and cost effective to produce

Rate how your organisation supports skills learning.

	Virtual	Relational	Physical	Aspirational
Jan 2032	4	4	4	4
Feb 2032	3	2	1	3
Mar 2032	5	3	4	4

This tool is adapted from the Skills Labyrinth tool designed by Tom Graves.
http://weblog.tetradian.com/2015/08/19/seven-sins-7-lost-in-the-learning-labyrinth/

56. People issues scenarios

How to have a balanced team
The Modes tool

Photograph source: Flickr, SKYRUN INC, CGI Office Joseph Chittenden

About this tool in brief
This version of the tool looks at the types of characteristics and skills needed to best fit a project's requirements.

The scenario
In this imagined scenario a multi-national investment firm has a major investment project. How best to approach this project has led the investment firm to evaluate the best skills for the project. The **Modes** tool is used to help find the skills needed to resolve the project, by imagining it is run by people using four **thinking modes**.

About this tool
If we imagine that the investment firm want to assemble a team to run the investment project, there are of course multiple ways of picking a team.
This version of the tool takes the approach of imagining that there are four **thinking modes** which are used to resolve projects: **The Scientist**, **The Builder**, **The Believer** and **The Artist**. Each of these has strengths and weaknesses.
This tool imagines that a project was run by people using one of these thinking modes. For example **The Believer** would follow rules consistently, but could run into trouble if they encountered unique situations.
In the last section of the tool we would '*cherry-pick*' the best from each of the four modes to create a '*dream team*'.
So in our investment project example we would have a team with an emphasis on the artist mode, under the guidance of the scientist mode to allow controlled innovation.
This tool is not used to find specific people with specific skills. Rather it is used to explore the skills which will be best suit the needs of your project.

In brief
The different modes also fit with the different parts of the SCAN tool *(see page 82)*:
1. The Scientist
2. The Believer
3. The Builder
4. The Artist
Each deals with different levels of complexity and time.

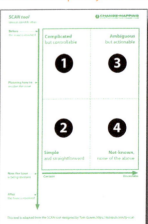

Modes tool

Mission identification:

Imagine your project was run with only *one* of these modes.

We run the project as a Scientist
"I verify the truth of things in relation to others".
"I make the unknown known and create rules".
"But I can want to continuously refine my evidence, delaying its use".

We run the project as a Builder
"I take what others have found and replicate them to resolve issues".
"I can adapt ideas to best resolve an issue through simple methods".
"But I prefer known reliable methods and I am unlikely to innovate".

We run the project as a Believer
"I follow the rules and deliver results consistently".
"I am reliable, dedicated and I stick to the plan".
"But I can become dependent on rules and without them I can become ineffective".

We run the project as an Artist
"I explore the unknown to see what's out there".
"I am highly innovative and come up with ideas that no one else could".
"But I tend not to stick to one thing and see it through".

Which combination of modes would best suit your project?

This tool is adapted from the Tetradian Swamp Metaphor, see:
http://weblog.tetradian.com/2012/08/12/sensemaking-modes-and-disciplines/

What is the best way to resolve issues? Stick to what you know or explore the unknown?

How to use this tool

How can this tool help you?
This version of the tool imagines that a project is run by people who use different **thinking modes**. Each mode has strengths and weaknesses. An important note is that this tool is not used to find specific people with skills, rather looking at what skills are needed to best suit a specific project.

What needs to be done before using this tool?
In this example the investment firm want to manage new energy investments for their client. This is the focus of a mission which will have its own **Mission Start** and **Context** Folder. It also needs to find out the best way to approach the investment project. This is explored using the **Modes** tool in the **Scope** folder.

How long would it take to complete a Modes tool-sheet?
In this example the investment firm took a few hours to complete the tool-sheet.

A brief guide to using the Modes tool

❶ Here the mission is stated. In our example the investment firm wants to manage an investment project for their client, part of that is looking at the most appropriate skills for managing the investment project.

❷ In this section you imagine that your project is run by people using four **thinking modes**. Each mode has strengths and weaknesses. For example, the **Artist mode** may find a unique investment opportunity that could be a game-changer or a real turkey.

❸ In this section you pick the best modes to suit your project. In our example a person running the project would use a combination of the **Scientist** and **Artist thinking modes**. This would allow them to be innovative, but run the project with rules to stop it becoming too out of control.

What other tools work well with this tool?

Ⓟ The **Leadership** tool would be useful here to strike a balance between rigid leadership and allowing autonomy. *(See page 48)*.

Ⓟ The **SCAN** tool can be useful here to gauge how each mode would react if less time was available to resolve the issue. *(See page 82)*.

Modes tool

Mission identification: How best to manage the investment in new energy projects for our clients?
> Explore the best team requirements to run the investment project.

Imagine your project was run with only *one* of these modes.

We run the project as a Scientist
"I verify the truth of things in relation to others".
"I make the unknown known and create rules".
"But I can want to continuously refine my evidence, delaying its use".

"I would have a solid evidence based approach to investing in new energy projects".

"But I might be too slow deciding which energy companies to invest in and our competitors might get ahead".

We run the project as a Builder
"I take what others have found and replicate them to resolve issues".
"I can adapt ideas to best resolve an issue through simple methods".
"But I prefer known reliable methods and I am unlikely to innovate".

"I would look at proven energy projects, which are known to generate reasonable returns in investment".

"While I look for proven energy projects I would most probably not do high risk projects which could create high rewards".

We run the project as a Believer
"I follow the rules and deliver results consistently".
"I am reliable, dedicated and stick to the plan".
"But I can become dependent on rules and without them I can become ineffective".

"If I am given clear rules and instructions, I will work tirelessly to find the best energy investment projects for our client"

"But without clear instructions I wouldn't know how to find energy investment projects".

We run the project as an Artist
"I explore the unknown to see what's out there".
"I am highly innovative and come up with ideas that no one else could".
"But I tend not to stick to one thing and see it through".

"I would look in unknown areas and may find a a game changer that no one else thought to look for".

"But I might waste time looking for a game-changer, that just doesn't exist".

Which combination of modes would best suit your project?

When we run this project, we would need to be self sufficient and able to hunt out the best opportunities. Therefore the Believer mode would most probably not be a good fit. The Builder mode would most probably not be bold enough. We think that a combination of the Artist and Scientist mode would work well. Being innovative but staying within set limits.

This tool is adapted from the Tetradian Swamp Metaphor, see:
http://weblog.tetradian.com/2012/08/12/sensemaking-modes-and-disciplines/

How to find out what is really happening
The SEMPER tool

Photograph source: Flickr, SKYRUNINC, CGI Office Joseph Christensen

The scenario
In this imagined scenario a multi-national investment firm has noticed a lack of client trust in their services.
The Malaysian headquarters believes that front-line staff are to blame, while the front-line staff feel under-valued.
The investment firm uses the **SEMPER** tool in an effort to find out the true state of the situation.

About this tool
This version of the tool is designed to take a snapshot of how the members of an organisation are functioning.
Often management has a different view of how the organisation is working compared to front-line staff.
Cost-cutting for example may seem logical from a managerial point of view but on the front-line cost-cutting can have radical effects.
The tool is made up of twenty-five questions such as:
Is the company's vision easy to understand and implement?
Are business relationships easily created and supported?
Is personal knowledge recognised and shared?
At the end of these questions you should have a score out of one hundred and twenty-five.
The tool shown here is a simplified version of the **SEMPER** tool. There is a more detailed book which goes into more depth about **SEMPER**. For more details visit:
http://tetradianbooks.com/2008/07/semper/

About this tool in brief
This version of SEMPER is used to measure staff member's ability to do work within an organisation. Rather than arbitrarily assigning blame, a more accurate picture can show what is actually happening.

The scores in brief
Adding up the scores *(see right)* shows how an organisation is functioning. Scores under **fifty** suggest the organisation has significant problems which need to be resolved urgently. Scores around **seventy-five** show an organisation which is functioning well and should be able to maintain that success.
Scores over **one hundred**, while impressive, are unlikely to be maintained for long before people buckle under the pressure.

SEMPER tool

Mission identification:

Context questions	C1	C2	C3	C4	C5
Scope questions	S1	S2	S3	S4	S5
Plan questions	P1	P2	P3	P4	P5
Action questions	A1	A2	A3	A4	A5
Review questions	R1	R2	R3	R4	R5

Total out of 125

C1: Our organisation's vision, values and purpose includes social and global concerns.
C2: Our organisation's vision, values and purpose inspire personal commitment by members.
C3: Our organisation's vision, values and purpose are clear, simple and easy to apply in practice.
C4: Our organisation's vision, values and purpose provide clear guidelines to manage change.
C5: Our organisation's vision, values and purpose anchor all aspects of the enterprise.

S1: Relationships support business purpose within our organisation.
S2: Personal element of relationships is supported within our organisation.
S3: Relationships and trust are easily created, supported and maintained within our organisation.
S4: Relationships are grounded in balanced *'fair exchange'* within our organisation.
S5: Relationships and *'feel'* help to bring everything together within our organisation.

P1: Knowledge and beliefs support business purpose within our organisation.
P2: Personal knowledge is recognised, supported and shared within our organisation.
P3: Support is provided for innovation, creativity and development of skills within our organisation.
P4: Knowledge provided is available, accurate and complete within our organisation.
P5: Knowledge supports the whole enterprise within our organisation.

A1: Tasks, skills, facilities and resources support purpose within our organisation.
A2: Skills and resources are of suitable quality for each task within our organisation.
A3: Work-processes are efficient and support enterprise performance within our organisation.
A4: Skills, resources and environment support consistent results within our organisation.
A5: Work-processes provide a focus for the whole enterprise within our organisation

R1: Metrics indicate when the enterprise is effective and *'on purpose'* within our organisation.
R2: Integration supports diversity of skills, background and experience within our organisation.
R3: Beliefs and business models support overall integration within our organisation.
R4: Everyone is involved in system-wide feedback and reflection within our organisation.
R5: Appropriate metrics support overall integration within our organisation.

This tool is adapted from the **SEMPER** tool designed by Tom Graves.
See: http://tetradian.com/tools/ecanvas/semperabout/

What is really happening inside an organisation?

How to use this tool

How can this tool help you?
This version of the tool is used to provide a snapshot of an organisation's ability *(chiefly of its staff)* to perform their jobs, so that any changes made are based on evidence and not assumptions. This is done by posing a set of questions and evaluating them based on a score out of one hundred and twenty five.

What needs to be done before using this tool?
In this example a mission is run to: *'Measure staff capability, because of a lack of client trust in our company'.*
So a small team using the standard *Change-mapping* system will run a mission. This tool is a **SCOPE** folder tool.
Before doing the **SEMPER** analysis the team should understand the context of the issue. Understanding the context would most likely show areas which need further investigation, which is where the **SEMPER** tool could help.

How long would it take to complete a SEMPER tool-sheet?
In this example, a sample of one hundred staff and management answered the questions with each sheet taking twenty minutes to fill in. Then a day to interpret all the results.

A brief guide to using SEMPER

❶ Note here the mission that the tool is being used for. For example exploring how an investment firm functions.

❷ These are the questions that need to be answered. For each question give your answer a score out of five: one meaning you strongly disagree, and five you strongly agree.

❸ Here you will place the scores for each question asked. For example in **C3** *(a Context question)* the responder has given a score of one out of five. So the responder strongly disagrees that the company's vision is easy to apply in practice.

❹ Here is the total out of one hundred and twenty five, so we can see that thirty nine shows there are problems.
The score on its own is good for a quick overview, but more useful is to see where things are going wrong such as in this example, the context questions suggest large problems with the insurance company's vision.

What other tools work well with this tool?
Π The **Visioning** tool can be useful to establish that the vision of the organisation is clear to everyone. *(See page 14).*
Σ The **Leadership** tool could be useful to help if the **SEMPER** tool reveals problems with staff morale. *(See page 48).*
Φ The **Knock-on effects** tool can act as a caution if any issues highlighted by **SEMPER** are not resolved. *(See page 68).*

SEMPER tool

Mission identification: **Measuring staff capability, because of a lack of client trust in our company**

		C1	C2	C3	C4	C5
Context questions	Π	1	1	1	1	1
Scope questions	Σ	S1 1	S2 3	S3 2	S4 2	S5 1
Plan questions		P1 2	P2 1	P3 1	P4 1	P5 1
Action questions		A1 1	A2 3	A3 2	A4 2	A5 2
Review questions	Φ	R1 2	R2 2	R3 2	R4 1	R5 2

Total out of 125: 39

C1: Our organisation's vision, values and purpose includes social and global concerns.
C2: Our organisation's vision, values and purpose inspire personal commitment by members.
C3: Our organisation's vision, values and purpose are clear, simple and easy to apply.
C4: Our organisation's vision, values and purpose provide clear guid...
C5: Our organisation's vision, values and purpose anchor all asp...

S1: Relationships support business purpose within our organisa...
S2: Personal element of relationships is supported within our or...
S3: Relationships and trust are easily created, supported and mai...
S4: Relationships are grounded in balanced *'fair exchange'* within...
S5: Relationships and *'feel'* help to bring everything together within our organisation.

P1: Knowledge and beliefs support business purpose within our organisation.
P2: Personal knowledge is recognised, supported and shared within our organisation.
P3: Support is provided for innovation, creativity and development of skills within our organisation.
P4: Knowledge provided is available, accurate and complete within our organisation.
P5: Knowledge supports the whole enterprise within our organisation.

A1: Tasks, skills, facilities and resources support purpose within our organisation.
A2: Skills and resources are of suitable quality for each task within our organisation.
A3: Work-processes are efficient and support enterprise performance within our organisation.
A4: Skills, resources and environment support consistent results within our organisation.
A5: Work-processes provide a focus for the whole enterprise within our organisation.

R1: Metrics indicate when the enterprise is effective and *'on purpose'* within our organisation.
R2: Integration supports diversity of skills, background and experience within our organisation.
R3: Beliefs and business models support overall integration within our organisation.
R4: Everyone is involved in system-wide feedback and reflection within our organisation.
R5: Appropriate metrics support overall integration within our organisation.

This tool is adapted from the **SEMPER** tool designed by Tom Graves.
See: *http://tetradian.com/tools/ecanvas/semperabout/*

64. People issues scenarios

How to find the story of an organisation
The NOTES tool

Photograph source: Flickr, Mike McBey, Monument Valley

About this tool in brief
What is an organisation's story? This version of the tool uses the metaphor of a film and all those involved in bringing it to the screen to describe a business story.

The scenario
In this imagined scenario, the Navajo Nation's Monument Valley Park, USA investigates if using Big Data could help understand visitor habits. So the park uses the **NOTES** tool to explore the relationships between people, processes and technology and how these combine to make the park's story.

About this tool
How issues are resolved by an organisation can be described through a spreadsheet, but this will only tell part of the *'story'*. This version of the **NOTES** tool takes the metaphor of a film and its production to tell a business story.
Any film will be made up of a director, producer, and actors. But then there are the multitudes of other people who are not in the spotlight, but just as vital, such as location scouts, caterers and of course the audience.
Using the **NOTES** tool, we can then apply the idea of a film crew to our example of the park in the USA.
The tool is split into groups who would be part of the park's story. Each role in a film can translate into a business context. By filling in each part of this tool, the story of who does what and why will start to appear. Understanding this will then help to see if Big Data would actually complement the story.
In our example we see that Big Data would be useful in reviewing visitor numbers, which in turn could be used to predict certain times of the year which might benefit from extra staff and park rangers.

NOTES tool

Mission identification:

Director   **Overall strategy**

Writer

Pre-production   **Marketing**

Advisors *(Experts)*   **Environmental**

Art department *(Design)*   **Transportation** *(Logistics)*   **IT**

Production *(Management)*

                                     Safety   **Casting** *(HR)*

                                     Legal

Cast   **Locations**   **Cyber security**

Camera, lighting, sound   **Props**
(General running of the organisation)   **Special effects**   **Sales**
                                     (Unusual circumstances)

                                     Security

Editing   **Accounts**   **Audience**

                                     Critics

This tool is adapted from a log written by Tom Graves:
http://weblog.tetradian.com/2013/06/10/notes-actors-agents-extras-in-enterprise/

Who are the key players inside an organisation's story?

How to use this tool

How can this tool help you?
This version of the tool uses the metaphor of a film production to describe all the people, props, locations, etc that are needed to tell an organisation's story. In this example, who are the actors, director, audience and others that are part of the park's story.
The tool breaks this down into sections, as well as looking at how Big Data would affect the overall story *(Yellow tabs, see diagram right).*

What needs to be done before using this tool?
This is a **Scope** folder tool which would support a mission to confirm if the park would benefit from using Big Data, before rushing to invest in a potentially expensive new system.

How long would it take to complete a NOTES tool-sheet?
In this example a small team took a few hours to sketch out the key parts of the story. The information found helped to confirm that Big Data would help the park.

A brief guide to using the NOTES tool

① Note here the mission that the tool is being used for. For example exploring how Big Data affects the park's story.

② This section looks at who creates the park's vision. An example might be the director who has an overall vision for the park.

③ This section looks at who explores options to achieve the park's vision. For example advisors and pre-production.

④ This section looks at who will create the plan to enact the vision for the park. For example casting *(Human resources)* or the art department *(Design)* who will create actual plans.

⑤ This section looks at who will enact the plan to achieve the park's vision. For example cast *(the park rangers)* and special effects *(who would deal with unusual circumstances such as a landslide).*

⑥ This section looks at who will review how the vision was enacted. For example the audience *(park visitors)* and critics *(reviewing how the plan was enacted).*

In our example the yellow tabs were added where the park felt that Big Data would complement the park's story.

What other tools work well with this tool?

Θ The **Visioning** tool can be used to identify the organisation's vision. *(See page 14).*

Λ The **Enterprise Canvas** tool can be used to explore how an organisation functions as a service. *(See page 18).*

☰ The **Service cycle** tool can be used to explore the customers' journey while using a service. *(See page 30).*

Σ The **Inside/Out** tool can be used to see how an organisation functions inside and out *(See page 40).*

NOTES tool

Mission identification: Using Big Data to map visitor habits in Monument Valley

Director
Navajo nation parks who manage four nature parks in south west USA.

Overall strategy
The Navajo nation parks vision for the parks.

Writer
The Navajo Nation who lead the overall strategy.

Big Data could help to verify the vision

Pre-production
Our strategy and marketing depts. come up with ideas for events in the park.

Marketing
Our internal marketing dept. does our online and printed marketing.

Advisors (Experts)
We have cultural advisors and we consult experts to help each department.

Environmental
We don't have a specific department but rather it is part of our core values and we consider environmental effects across the whole park.

Big Data could help here

Art department (Design)
Our internal marketing dept.

Production (Management)
The management team is based in the park and is made up of thirty people.

Transportation (Logistics)
We have a fleet of twenty 4WD vehicles

Safety
We follow national guidelines.

Legal
We use an external legal team based in Los Angeles.

IT
Our IT is performed by an external unit based in Seattle.

Casting (HR)
Our management team based in the park is also involved with human resources.

Cast
Rangers, store staff.

Camera, lighting, sound
(General running of the organisation)
Our management team deals with the day to day running of the park.

Locations
Navajo Nation's Monument Valley Park.

Props
Uniforms, souvenirs.

Special effects
(Unusual circumstances)
We have a disaster recovery plan in place.

Security
Security is run by our rangers.

Cyber security
Our external IT dept looks after cyber security.

Sales
Our external IT team runs our e-booking system

Big Data could help here

Editing
We have monthly meetings with strategy, management and accounts.

Big Data could help here

Accounts
Our management team has two dedicated members who perform all accounting tasks.

Audience
All park visitors, potential park visitors

Critics
Past visitors, journalists

This tool is adapted from a log written by Tom Graves:
http://weblog.tetradian.com/2013/06/10/notes-actors-agents-extras-in-enterprise/

68. People issues scenarios

How to prepare for unexpected knock-on effects
The Knock-on effects tool

Photograph source: Flickr, Mike McBey. CGI Train, Joseph Chittenden

About this tool in brief
This tool is used to start discussions about the potential unexpected knock-on effects of resolving issues.

The scenario
In this scenario we can imagine that a massive demand for train services in central Spain has led to calls for a rush investment in a new high speed rail network.
Before considering investing in such a mega project the train operator examines the potential knock-on effects.

About this tool
Risk management is commonly used to try to analyse and manage the potential risk of resolving an issue.
This tool looks at potential *unexpected* knock-on effects of resolving an issue. When an organisation is under pressure to resolve an issue immediately, possible unexpected knock-on effects may seem a low priority. This tool aims to start discussions by exploring the complex and random interactions of unexpected and seemingly unconnected events.
This tool shows with just twenty-four individual knock-on effects, when combined just four times, they can lead to over fifteen hundred combinations of knock-on effects.
By considering likely effects and less likely higher impact events then any solution they choose should be better 'future proofed'.
The need for this has been shown many times, such as the introduction of cane toads to eradicate beetles in Australia. Instead of the cane toads eating the beetles, the cane toads ignored the beetles and began to have widespread negative impact on native wildlife.

Knock-on effects tool

CHANGE→MAPPING
CONNECTING BUSINESS TOOLS TO MANAGE CHANGE

Mission identification:

Potential general knock-on effects of _____

⚀ Roll one dice, note result
01. Effects on air quality
02. Climate effects
03. Effects on delays
04. Effects on sustain.*
05. Service effects
06. Effects on time

⚀⚁ Roll two dice, note result
02. Climate effects
03. Effects on delays
04. Effects on sustain.*
05. Service effects
06. Effects on time
07. Effects on costs
08. Effects on staff
09. Effects on managers
10. Effects on clients
11. Effects on leadership
12. Effects on revenue

⚀⚁⚂ Roll three dice, note result
03. Effects on delays
04. Effects on sustain.*
05. Service effects
06. Effects on time
07. Effects on costs
08. Effects on staff
09. Effects on managers
10. Effects on clients
11. Effects on leadership
12. Effects on revenue
13. Effects on security
14. Effect on DR**
15. Effects on IT
16. Effects on environ.***
17. Effects on pollution
18. Effects on waste

⚀⚁⚂⚃ Roll four dice, note result
04. Effects on sustain.*
05. Service effects
06. Effects on time
07. Effects on costs
08. Effects on staff
09. Effects on managers
10. Effects on clients
11. Effects on leadership
12. Effects on revenue
13. Effects on security
14. Effect on DR**
15. Effects on IT
16. Effects on environ.***
17. Effects on pollution
18. Effects on waste
19. Effects on H & S****
20. Effects on values
21. Effects on freedom
22. Information effects
23. Effects on tech.
24. Effects on world

Potential general knock-on effects of _____

which leads to

which leads to

which leads to

*Sustainability
** Disaster recovery
***Natural environment
****Health and safety

Once you set something in motion, do you know what will happen next?

How to use this tool

How can this tool help you?
This version of the tool is used to start discussions about how prepared your organisation is, to deal with the potential unexpected knock-on effects of resolving an issue.

What needs to be done before using this tool?
In this example the train operator is keen to invest in a new railway, but rather than rushing to a plan they want to examine risk with standard tools. They also explore unexpected events with this tool which is used in the **Scope** folder.

How long would it take to complete a Knock-on effects tool-sheet?
The actual sheet would in this example take a few minutes to complete. In our example, the train operator would likely take a few hours examining potential-knock on effects in more detail to see how they would deal with them.

A brief guide to using the Knock-on effects tool

1. Note here the mission that the tool is being used for. For example exploring investing in a new rail network.
2. Roll one dice and note the result, in this example *'effects on sustainability'*.
3. Roll two dice and note the result, in this example *'effects on staff'*.
4. Roll three dice and note the result, in this example *'effects on service's*.
5. Roll four dice and note the result, in this example *'effects on information'*.
6. In this section combine all the four results together. This is the new scenario which has been generated randomly. For example *'Building the railway leads to effects on sustainability, which leads to effects on staff, which leads to effects on services, which leads to effects on information'.* The team then examines the knock-on effects of all these factors, which can have positive and negative effects on the overall scenario. After this stage the team would then reconsider how they would deal with unexpected knock-on effects. This could be done by using some of the other tools in this book to obtain more information.

What other tools work well with this tool?
- The **Service cycle** tool can be used to explore the customers' journey while using a service. *(See page 30).*
- The **Leadership** tool could be used to explore leadership issues within the organisation. *(See page 48).*
- The **SCAN** tool can be useful here to explore how time can affect resolving issues. *(See page 82).*

Knock-on effects tool

①

CHANGE→MAPPING
CONNECTING BUSINESS TOOLS TO MANAGE CHANGE

Mission identification: *Potential knock-on effects of a new high speed rail network between Madrid and Valladolid*

Potential general knock-on effects of *Building a new high speed rail network between Madrid and Valladolid*

⚀ Roll one dice, note result

01. Effects on air quality
02. Climate effects

03. Effects on delays
04. Effects on sustain.*

05. Service effects ⊖
06. Effects on time

②

⚀⚁ Roll two dice, note result

02. Climate effects
03. Effects on delays
04. Effects on sustain.*
05. Service effects ⊖

06. Effects on time ☰
07. Effects on costs
08. Effects on staff
09. Effects on managers

10. Effects on clients ∧
11. Effects on leadership
12. Effects on revenue

③

⚀⚁⚂ Roll three dice, note result

03. Effects on delays
04. Effects on sustain.*
05. Service effects ⊖
06. Effects on time ☰
07. Effects on costs
08. Effects on staff

09. Effects on managers
10. Effects on clients
11. Effects on leadership ∧
12. Effects on revenue
13. Effects on security
14. Effect on DR**

15. Effects on IT
16. Effects on environ.***
17. Effects on pollution
18. Effects on waste

④

⚀⚁⚂⚃ Roll four dice, note result

04. Effects on sustain.*
05. Service effects ⊖
06. Effects on time ☰
07. Effects on costs
08. Effects on staff
09. Effects on managers
10. Effects on clients
11. Effects on leadership ∧

12. Effects on revenue
13. Effects on security
14. Effect on DR**
15. Effects on IT
16. Effects on environ.***
17. Effects on pollution
18. Effects on waste

19. Effects on H & S****
20. Effects on values
21. Effects on freedom
22. Information effects
23. Effects on tech.
24. Effects on world

⑤

Potential general knock-on effects of *Building a new high speed rail network between Madrid and Valladolid*

⑥

⚀ *Effects on sustainability, such as reducing pollution compared to cars*

which leads to

⚁ *Effects on staff, such as fatigue on longer journeys*

which leads to

⚂ *Effects on service, such as increased need for extra staff*

which leads to

⚃ *Effects on information, such as better understanding of customer habits on-board*

*Sustainability
** Disaster recovery
***Natural environment
****Health and safety

Chapter 3: Scenarios for planning issues
Plan folder tools in action

NOTE
All the scenarios are hypothetical and fiction. The organisations mentioned are used to illustrate a specific issue to better describe how the tools could be used.

Downloadable tools
Available at the time of writing to download are PDFs and PowerPoint slides of the tools shown in this chapter.
https://www.changemappingbook.com/plan-tools

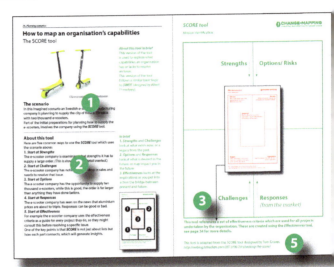

About these tools
In this chapter we look at tools used to plan the resolution of issues or enterprises.

In the first *Change-mapping* book a simple **Plan** tool was used, here we look at four new **Plan** tools.

The tools in this chapter are used to:
- Map an organisation's capabilities to resolve an issue.
- Establish strategies for resolving unknown issues.
- Map the uncertainties of resolving an issue.
- Pick a tool to explore, address or resolve an issue.

The scenarios
In order to show how these new **Plan** tools work, we have created four scenarios. Each scenario has a real world issue which uses one of the tools to explore, address or resolve the issue.

It is important to note that any of the tools could be used in any scenario and are not limited to only being used within that specific scenario.

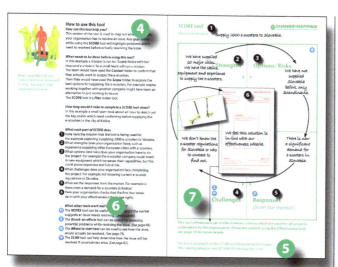

How to use this chapter
How can these tools help you?
These tools are used to explore the planning issues within an issue or enterprise. This will be vital when resolving issues by fully understanding how it will be resolved.

What needs to be done before using these tools?
You should read the first *Change-mapping* book, as this will show you how everything works and how to add more detailed tools, such as the ones shown in this chapter.

A brief guide to using this chapter
Each tool is discussed over four pages
- A scenario showing the *Change-mapping* tool in use exploring a real world issue.
- A general description of the tool discussing when and what it is used for.
- A blank version of the tool which can be copied and used in your own *Change-mapping* missions.
- Instructions showing how to use each tool including what needs to be done *before* using the tool.
- A link to where you can find out more information about the tool online.
- A list of other tools in the book which work well with the tool shown.
- A filled-in example of the tool which uses the scenario to help you understand how to use the tool.

Using these tools in a Change-mapping mission

1. Set up a mission to explore or resolve an issue, with a **Mission start folder**.

2. Use a **Context folder** to explore the context of the issue.

2. Use a **Scope folder** to explore the people issues.

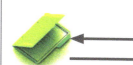

2. Use a **Plan folder** to explore the planning issues. If the basic Plan folder doesn't generate enough information, add one of the tools from this chapter, which best fit your requirements.

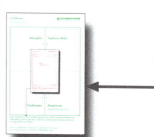

How to map an organisation's capabilities
The SCORE tool

CGI e-scooter, Joseph Chittenden

About this tool in brief
This version of the tool is used to explore what capabilities an organisation has or lacks to resolve an issue.
*This version of the tool follows a similar basic logic to **SWOT** (designed by Albert Humphrey).*

The scenario
In this imagined scenario an Swedish e-scooter manufacturing company is planning to supply the city of Košice, Slovakia with two thousand e-scooters.
Part of the initial preparations for planning how to supply the e-scooters, involves the company using the **SCORE** tool.

About this tool
Here are five common ways to use the **SCORE** tool which uses the scenario above:

1. Start at Strengths
The e-scooter company is examining what strengths it has to supply a large order. *(This is shown in more detail overleaf.)*

2. Start at Challenges
The e-scooter company has noticed a large drop in sales and needs to resolve that issue.

3. Start at Options
The e-scooter company has the opportunity to supply ten thousand e-scooters, while this is good, the order is far larger then anything they have done before.

4. Start at Responses
The e-scooter company has seen on the news that aluminium prices are about to triple. Responses can be good or bad.

5. Start at Effectiveness
For example the e-scooter company uses the effectiveness criteria as a guide for *every* project they do, so they might consult this before resolving a specific issue.
One of the key points is that **SCORE** is not just about lists but how each part connects, which will generate insights.

In brief
*1. **Strengths** and **Challenges** look at what exists now, or a legacy from the past.*
*2. **Options** and **Responses** look at what is desired in the future, or may impact you in the future*
*3. **Effectiveness** looks at the implications as you put into action the bridge between present and future.*

SCORE tool

Mission identification:

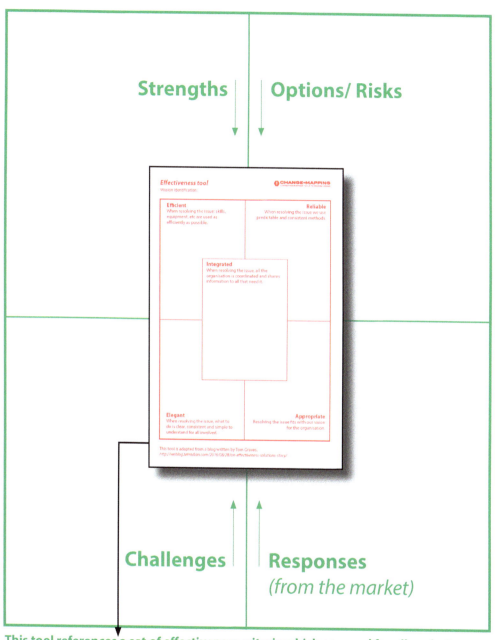

Strengths **Options/ Risks**

Challenges **Responses**
(from the market)

This tool references a set of effectiveness criteria which are used for all projects undertaken by the organisation. These are created using the *Effectiveness* tool, see page 34 for more details.

This tool is adapted from the SCORE tool designed by Tom Graves.
http://weblog.tetradian.com/2013/06/29/checking-the-score/

What capabilities do you have to resolve an issue, and do they stay true to your organisation's vision?

How to use this tool

How can this tool help you?
This version of the tool is used to map out what capabilities your organisation has to resolve an issue. Any gaps found while using the **SCORE** tool will highlight problems which need to resolved before actually resolving the issue.

What needs to be done before using this tool?
In this example a mission is run to: *'Supply Košice with two thousand e-scooters'.* So a small team will run a mission.
The team would have used the **Context** folder to confirm that they actually want to supply the e-scooters.
Then they would have used the **Scope** folder to explore the best options for supplying the e-scooters. For example maybe working together with another company might have been an alternative to just working in-house.
The **SCORE** tool is a **Plan** folder tool.

How long would it take to complete a SCORE tool-sheet?
In this example a small team took about an hour to sketch out the key points which need confirming before supplying the e-scooters to the city of Košice.

What each part of SCORE does
❶ Note here the mission that the tool is being used for. For example exploring supplying 2000 e-scooters to Slovakia.
❷ What strengths does your organisation have, such as experience supplying other European cities with e-scooters.
❸ What options *(and risks)* does your organisation have to do the project. For example the e-scooter company could invest in new equipment which increases their capabilities, but this could prove expensive and full of risk.
❹ What challenges does your organisation face completing the project. For example not knowing current e-scooter regulations in Slovakia.
❺ What are the responses from the market. For example is there even a demand for e-scooters in Košice?
❻ Here your organisation checks that the first four boxes tie-in with your effectiveness criteria *(see right)*.

What other tools work well with this tool?
Π The **NOTES** tool can be useful to understand if the market suggests an issue needs resolving. *(See page 64)*.
Σ The **Knock-on effects** tool can be useful for assessing potential problems while resolving the issue. *(See page 68)*.
Φ The **Where to start tool** can be used to see how the issue would actually be resolved. *(See page 78)*.
Ψ The **SCAN** tool can help determine how the issue will be resolved if uncertainties arise. *(See page 82)*.

SCORE tool

Mission identification: Supply 2000 e-scooters to Slovakia.

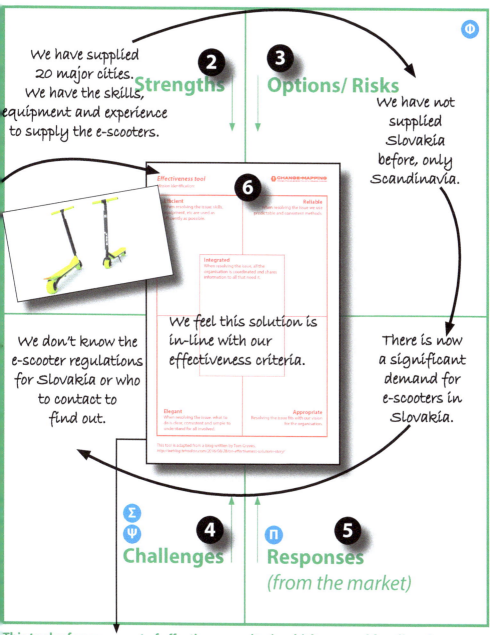

2 Strengths
We have supplied 20 major cities. We have the skills, equipment and experience to supply the e-scooters.

3 Options/ Risks
We have not supplied Slovakia before, only Scandinavia.

There is now a significant demand for e-scooters in Slovakia.

We feel this solution is in-line with our effectiveness criteria.

4 Challenges
We don't know the e-scooter regulations for Slovakia or who to contact to find out.

5 Responses *(from the market)*

This tool references a set of effectiveness criteria which are used for all projects undertaken by the organisation. These are created using the *Effectiveness* tool, see page 34 for more details.

This tool is adapted from the SCORE tool designed by Tom Graves.
http://weblog.tetradian.com/2013/06/29/checking-the-score/

How to resolve an unknown issue
The Where to start? tool

Photograph source: Wikipedia, Martin St-Amant.
CGI Binoculars, Joseph Chittenden

About this tool in brief
This version of the tool is used to break down exactly how an issue will be resolved.

The scenario
In this imagined scenario a New York, USA based design agency want to promote their new binoculars.
They decide to photograph them on the Salar de Uyuni salt-flats of Bolivia. But they have no real idea how to attempt the photo-shoot, so the agency use the **Where to start** tool, to get practical ideas flowing.

About this tool
If we use the example of the team trying to plan a photo-shoot in Bolivia, it can be daunting to know where to start. The **Where to start** tool is used in these types of situations. We can imagine that the design agency are sat in their office with blank faces not knowing what to do. So they use the tool to get conversations started.
As they work through the questions a broad picture about how to approach the photo-shoot should start to appear.
Any gaps can be filled by using other tools such as the **Value** tool *(see page 6)*, this would hep them identify that authentic photographs would take priority over generic 'staged' shoots which would not support the brand.
At the end of the process they should be able to have a much better plan of action about how to get to Bolivia, run the photo-shoot and take the photographs they need.
This is preferable to rushing to Bolivia and then trying to solve unexpected issues in real time. The **SCAN** tool deals with addressing unexpected events before they happen *(see page 82 for more details)*.

Where to start tool

Mission identification:

What are you trying to resolve?
Why does it need to be resolved?
When does it need to be resolved?
What are the deliverables?
What information is required?
What skills are required?
What equipment is required?
How does this support our brand?
Where will it be resolved?
What could go wrong?
What is the budget to resolve the issue?
What safety measures are in place while resolving the issue?
Who will resolve the issue?
How will the resolution be stored, eg information, product?
What needs to be done first and in what order?

This tool is adapted from the THIS game designed by Tom Graves.
http://weblog.tetradian.com/2011/10/29/this-exploratory-game-for-service-oriented-ea/

Knowing where to start can sometimes be tricky.

How to use this tool

How can this tool help you?
This version of the tool is designed to generate ideas.
In this example when nobody knows where to start planning a product photo-shoot on the Salar de Uyuni salt-flats of Bolivia.

What needs to be done before using this tool?
In this example the design agency would run a mission confirming why they want to promote the new binoculars. This would be done in the **Context** folder.
In the **Scope** folder they would explore different options such as photographing the binoculars in Canada.
Once they confirmed that Bolivia would be a good place to photograph the binoculars, they would use the **Plan** folder *(where this tool is used)* to work out how they would actually do the photo-shoot. In this example they have no idea, so they use the **Where to start?** tool.

How long would it take to complete a Where to start? tool-sheet?
In this example the design agency took about an hour to start working out how they would photograph their binoculars.

A brief guide to using the Where to start? tool

❶ Note here the mission that the tool is being used for, such as planning a photo-shoot in Bolivia.

❷ This tool works by posing you a set of questions.
In our example the design agency goes through the questions to help them start to work out the broad details about how they will photograph the binoculars.
For example, one of the questions is:
'What information is required?' They would logically need to know how to get *to* Salar de Uyuni in Bolivia.
This would then lead to working out how *long* it would take to get to there and so on. So the questions act as conversation starters.

What other tools work well with this tool?

- Π The **Value** tool is useful here to establish what is valued, which will affect how the issue is resolved. *(See page 6)*.
- Σ The **Sense-making** tool works well with this tool, knowing what the issue is before trying resolve it. *(See page 10)*.
- Φ The **Modes** tool can be useful for looking at the best team to resolve the issue. *(See page 56)*.
- Ψ The **Knock-on effects** tool can show the potential consequences of resolving the issue without proper plans. *(See page 68)*.

Where to start tool

Mission identification: How to do a photo-shoot on the Salar de Uyuni saltflats of Bolivia

What are you trying to resolve?
How to photograph our new Binoculars on Salar de Uyuni salt-flats, Bolivia.

Why does it need to be resolved?
We need to promote our new binoculars to recoup development costs.

When does it need to be resolved?
Within two months (WHEN IS BEST TIME TO GO?).

What are the deliverables?
High quality photographs of the binoculars.

What information is required?
How to get to the salt-flats, lighting conditions.

What skills are required?
People used to desert conditions, can operate photographic equipment.

What equipment is required?
Binoculars, camera, tripod, power. (WHAT ABOUT TRANSPORT?)

How does this support our brand?
It will show our binoculars in their intended environment.

Where will it be resolved?
Salar de Uyuni salt-flats, Bolivia.

What could go wrong?
Cameras fail, bad weather, trouble travelling.

What is the budget to resolve the issue?
Equipment budget, travel budget, staff budget, supplies budget for one week.

What safety measures are in place while resolving the issue?
We will use a local guide, take extra supplies, 4WD vehicle.

Who will resolve the issue?
We will send our marketing team including Javier who is from Bolivia.

How will the resolution be stored, eg information, product?
The photographs will be stored on our cloud servers.

What needs to be done first and in what order?
Contact local guide, based on what they say purchase equipment and flights.

This tool is adapted from the THIS game designed by Tom Graves.
http://weblog.tetradian.com/2011/10/29/this-exploratory-game-for-service-oriented-ea/

How to reduce uncertainty
The SCAN tool

Photograph source: Wikipedia, Asco. CGI Dump truck, Joseph Chittenden

About this tool in brief
This version of the tool is used before resolving an issue, to find out what is known and what isn't when resolving that issue.

The scenario
In this imagined scenario a copper mine in Namibia is relocating. Part of this complex project includes moving the massive dump trucks. The mine uses the **SCAN** tool to explore the uncertainties of relocating the dump trucks, in terms of complexity and time. Once this was done the mine would integrate what was found with the rest of the mine relocation.

About this tool
If we use the example of moving the copper mine trucks, it would seem best to use a GANTT chart.
A GANTT chart assumes that everything is known about how to resolve an issue, but what about the unknowns?
What happens if an unexpected event happens at the last minute? This version of the **SCAN** tool is used to counter these types of problems. It asks a team to put what is known about the solving of the issue into the *'simple'* section, what is complicated into the *'complicated'* section and so on.
The further to the right in the tool, the more uncertain something is. The aim is to explore the unknowns *(Using the* ***Sense-making*** *tool can help, see page 10)* and turn them into knowns, before actually trying to move the copper mine trucks.
All the above assumes the copper mine has an infinite amount of time to move the trucks, but what if they have a limited amount of time? Time is introduced on the left of the **SCAN** tool. Reduced time can turn a simple action into a complicated action.
So by getting a more detailed idea of *how* to move the trucks, *before* they move the trucks, they should be less likely to run into unexpected problems.

In brief
An important note about **SCAN** is that the dashed lines are not static *(shown with black arrows, below).*
Often your **SCAN** tool will start with many unknowns before changing to look more like the **SCAN** tool shown on the right.

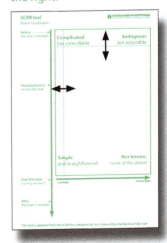

SCAN tool

Mission identification:

Before ➔
the issue is resolved

Planning how to ➔
resolve the issue

Now the issue ➔
is being resolved

After ➔
the issue is resolved

Complicated
but controllable

Ambiguous
but actionable

Simple
and straightforward

Not-known,
none of the above

Certain ➔ **Uncertain**

This tool is adapted from the SCAN tool designed by Tom Graves. *https://leanpub.com/tp-scan*

When trying to resolve something, what are the uncertainties and complexities?

How to use this tool

How can this tool help you?
This version of the tool is used to explore the uncertainties of resolving an issue, in terms of complexity and time. The tool acts as a cross-check so that when an issue is resolved, unexpected events don't cause problems.

What needs to be done before using this tool?
In this example the mine has confirmed they want to relocate, in the **Context** folder of a *'Relocate the mine mission'.* Such a large project would be split into many parts, each needing planning*. Here we look at just moving the dump trucks, with its own **Plan** folder, where the **SCAN** tool would be used.
See the first Change-mapping book (Page 102) for details about running larger and more complex missions.

How long would it take to complete a SCAN tool-sheet?
The **SCAN** tool in this example would take a couple of hours to work through all the potential problems.

A brief guide to using SCAN
❶ Note here the mission that the tool is being used for. For example planning to relocate dump trucks in Namibia.
❷ **Simple** tasks are placed here, such as hiring the logistics company to move the dump trucks.
❸ **Complicated** tasks are placed here, such as confirming the roads are wide enough for the dump trucks.
❹ **Ambiguous** parts of the project are placed here, such as how long will the relocation take, once this is known then it can be moved to the simple section.
❺ **Not-known** factors such as dust-storms which are hard to predict in real time, are placed here.
❻ This arrow introduces *'time'.* It acts as a countdown to project start, what needs sorting and when.
❼ This arrow shows the further to the right of the matrix, the more complex the task is.
❽ This dashed line is the *'boundary of effective certainty'* which can move right to left depending on certainty.
❾ This dashed line is the *'transition from plan to action'* which can move up and down depending on time required.

What other tools work well with this tool?
Σ The **Sense-making** tool can confirm that what is said to be *'simple and straight forward'* really is. *(See page 10).*
Φ The **Where to start** tool can be used to plan how to resolve an issue *(See page 82).*

SCAN tool

Mission identification: **Relocating the Copper Mine Dump Trucks in Namibia**

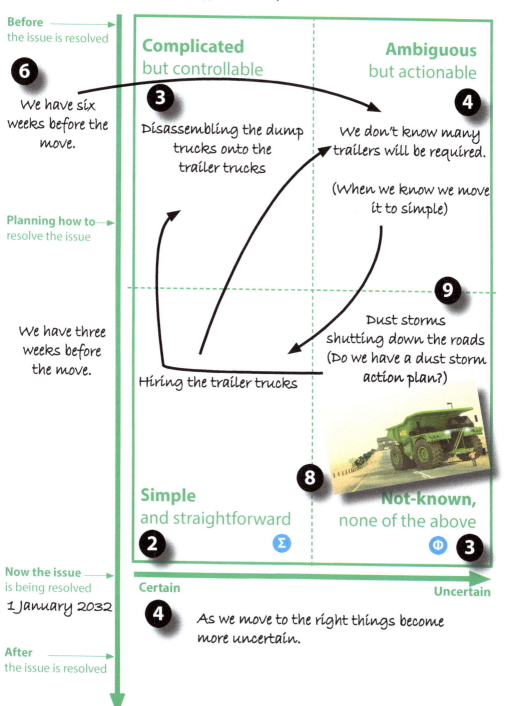

Before the issue is resolved

6 We have six weeks before the move.

Complicated but controllable

3 Disassembling the dump trucks onto the trailer trucks

Ambiguous but actionable

4 We don't know many trailers will be required.

(When we know we move it to simple)

Planning how to resolve the issue

We have three weeks before the move.

Hiring the trailer trucks

9 Dust storms shutting down the roads (Do we have a dust storm action plan?)

Simple and straightforward

2 Σ

Not-known, none of the above

8 Φ **3**

Now the issue is being resolved
1 January 2032

Certain → Uncertain

4 As we move to the right things become more uncertain.

After the issue is resolved

This tool is adapted from the SCAN tool designed by Tom Graves. https://leanpub.com/tp-scan

How to choose a new tool
The Tool finder tool

Photograph source: Flickr, David Figuera, www.twin-loc.fr
CGI Train, Joseph Chittenden

The Scenario
In this imagined scenario a Spanish train operator wants to better understand how their customers interact with the services they provide. But they are not sure if a tool exists to suit their needs and how to find such a tool. They decide to use the **Tool finder** tool to help them narrow down potential tools that could help.

About this tool
In our scenario the train operator knows roughly what they want to achieve, but they don't know if there is a tool that can do what they want. The **Tool finder** tool works in the same way as the **Where to start?** tool *(see page 78)*. In that it can not possibly ask every relevant question to suit every context. Rather it aims to *start* conversations about how to resolve your issue. With this tool the first thing to do is to specify *what* you want a new tool to do. Then see if such a tool exists. Usually, especially with the internet, you can find what you need. Then the next step is to see if you can *use* the tool. In our scenario *(see overleaf for more details)* the train operator found that CRM software matched their specification. Once they found that CRM software existed, then they needed to work out how to actually use it. So the **Tool finder** posed a basic set of questions so they could get up and running. As with the other tools in this book, the tool works more effectively when networked with other tools. This way you can gather extra information when required. The instructions mention some specific tools which can help you further.

About this tool in brief
This version of the tool is used to find and setup a new business tool.

In brief
Choosing and using a tool mirrors how *Change-mapping* works *(see page iii)*:
Mission Start, You have an issue you need to resolve.
Context, What is the context for this tool, eg it is a strategy tool used for business.
Scope, What are the limits of what it can do and who can use it?
Plan, What instructions and setup does it need before you can use it?
Action, The time where you actually use the tool.
Review, Where you review if the tool worked as intended.
Mission End, Was the issue successfully resolved?

Tool finder tool

Mission identification:

1. What do you need your tool to do?
Write specification then go to 2, if you can not, then go to 15.

2. Do you know if a tool exists which meets your needs?
If yes go to 5, if you do not, then go to 3.

3. Do you know how to find such a tool?
If yes find the tool and then go to 5, if you do not know then go to 4.

4. Can you ask an expert or find out such a tool on the internet/book/etc?
If yes, obtain information and go to 2, if you can not, then go to 15.

5. Do you know what information is required to use the tool?
If yes, obtain information and go to 6, if you do not know, then go to 14.

6. Do you know what skills are required to use the tool?
If yes, obtain information and go to 7, if you do not know, then go to 14.

7. Do you know what equipment is required to use the tool?
If yes, obtain information and go to 8, if you do not know, then go to 14.

8. Do you know what location is required to use the tool?
If yes, obtain information and go to 9, if you do not know, then go to 14.

9. Do you know what much time do you need to use the tool?
If yes, obtain information and go to 10, if you do not know, then go to 14.

10. Do you know what could go wrong while using the tool?
If yes, obtain information and go to 11, if you do not know, then go to 14.

11. Do you know what is the budget required to use the tool?
If yes, obtain information and go to 12, if you do not know, then go to 14.

12. Do you know a way to record the tool being used for future reference?
If yes, obtain information and go to 13, if you do not know, then go to 14.

13. Do you know who will use the tool?
If yes, obtain information and go to 16, if you do not know, then go to 14.

14. Can you ask an expert or find out on the internet/book/etc?
If yes, obtain information and go to 2, if you can not, then go to 15.

15. If you fail to find the information you need, try adding more detail to the specification, see the instructions about tools which can help.

16. Add any other steps you require before using the tool you are about to use, and then use it!

Where is the tool you need? And do you know how to use it?

How to use this tool

How can this tool help you?
This version of the tool is designed to generate ideas about how to find and effectively use new business tools.
In this example a Spanish train operator wants to understand more about their customers.

What needs to be done before using this tool?
Most probably the most important thing that needs to be done before using this tool, is to know why you need to find a specific tool. Therefore a **Nested mission*** would be set up. Just like a regular mission you would set the context and scope of why you need a new tool. The **Tool finder** tool has here been shown as a **Plan** folder tool, although it could be used in other folders, if required.
*See the first Change-mapping book, page 114 for information about Nested missions and page 92 of this book.

How long would it take to complete a Tool finder tool-sheet?
In this example the train operator took a few hours to start working out how to find a new tool and what was needed to use it.

A brief guide to using the Tool finder tool
❶ Note here the mission that the **Tool finder** tool is being used for. For example to find and use a new tool to suit the train operator's needs.
❷ Next, start at question one and work your way down to part sixteen. As shown in the example *(see right)* answering the questions will involve jumping around the tool-sheet. Once you get to part sixteen you should be better prepared to find and use the tool you need.
❸ In this section it suggests adding more detail to your tool's specification. The tools shown with the blue circles can help.

What other tools work well with this tool?
- **Θ** The basic tool set shown in the first *Change-mapping* book *(page 62)* can help with general questions about tools.
- **Λ** The **Sense-making** tool works well with this tool, to know what the issue is before trying resolve it. *(See page 10)*.
- **Π** The **Leadership** tool could be used to explore the leadership needed, when using the new tool. *(See page 48)*.
- **Σ** The **Knock-on effects** tool can show the potential consequences of resolving the issue. *(See page 68)*.
- **Φ** The **Where to start** tool can be used to plan how to resolve an issue. *(See page 78)*.
- **Ψ** The **SCAN** tool can help determine how the issue will be resolved if uncertainties arise. *(See page 82)*.

Tool finder tool

(1)

CHANGE→MAPPING
CONNECTING BUSINESS TOOLS TO MANAGE CHANGE

Mission identification: We need to find a tool which can help us better understand customer interactions with our trains.

(2)

1. What do you need your tool to do?
Write specification then go to 2, if you can not, then go to 15.

We need to find a tool which can integrate and automate sales, marketing, and customer support.

Θ Λ Φ

2. Do you know if a tool exists which meets your needs?
If yes go to 5, if you do not, then go to 3.

At this time we don't know if such a tool exists

3. Do you know how to find such a tool?
If yes find the tool and then go to 5, if you do not know, then go to 4.

Not really, maybe the internet can help?

4. Can you ask an expert or find out such a tool on the internet/book/etc?
If yes, obtain information and go to 2, if you can not, then go to 15.

We found a tool called CRM which looks promising.

5. Do you know what information is required to use the tool?
If yes, obtain information and go to 6, if you do not know, then go to 14.

We found usage information on the internet easily

6. Do you know what skills are required to use the tool?
If yes, obtain information and go to 7, if you do not know, then go to 14.

Π

A tutorial online showed us what skills are needed.

7. Do you know what equipment is required to use the tool?
If yes, obtain information and go to 8, if you do not know, then go to 14.

There seem two main types of software, we chose type 1.

8. Do you know what location is required to use the tool?
If yes, obtain information and go to 9, if you do not know, then go to 14.

We now know this.   We don't know this.

9. Do you know what much time do you need to use the tool? Ψ
If yes, obtain information and go to 10, if you do not know, then go to 14.

We will trial it for 6 months.

10. Do you know what could go wrong while using the tool? Σ
If yes, obtain information and go to 11, if you do not know, then go to 14.

We ran risk assessment.

11. Do you know what is the budget required to use the tool?
If yes, obtain information and go to 12, if you do not know, then go to 14.

We are aware of budget requirements.

12. Do you know a way to record the tool being used for future reference? Θ
If yes, obtain information and go to 13, if you do not know, then go to 14.

We are looking into this.

13. Do you know who will use the tool? Π
If yes, obtain information and go to 16, if you do not know, then go to 14.

We have set up a preliminary team.

14. Can you ask an expert or find out on the internet/book/etc?
If yes, obtain information and go to 2, if you can not, then go to 15.

We spoke to an expert, who set up the CRM software in-house.

15. If you fail to find the information you need, try adding more detail to the specification, see the instructions about tools which can help.

(3)

16. Add any other steps you require before using the tool you are about to use, and then use it!

We will begin to use the CRM software next week.

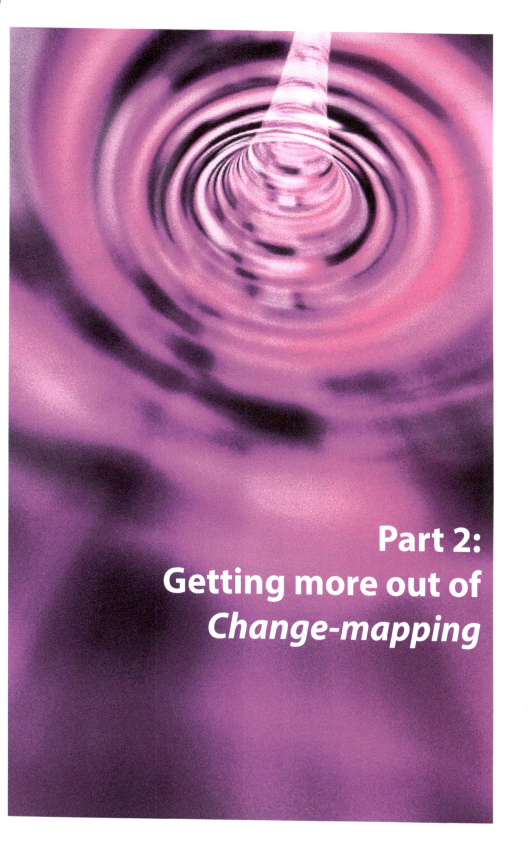

Part 2:
Getting more out of
Change-mapping

Chapter 4: How to run a Linked mission
Two missions using every Tetradian tool in this book

NOTE
Throughout the chapter the map references pages from this and the first Change-mapping book.
For example:
Context Folder
(Book 1, page 22)
Book 1 is the first Change-mapping book.
Book 2 is this book.

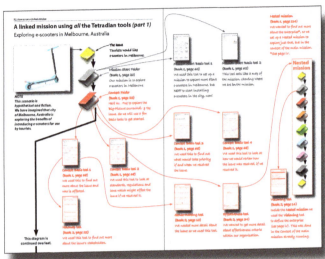

About this chapter
Now you are familiar with the new tools shown in this book we will show you how they can be used altogether.
We have done this by showing a **Linked mission*** from start to finish with every tool, including the basic tools shown in the first *Change-mapping* book.
A **Linked mission** is where two or more missions are connected to explore, address or resolve an issue.
We show the Linked mission using a scenario.
In our imagined scenario the city of Melbourne, Australia has received calls from tourists to introduce e-scooters. They want to look into this further as would appear to be a good idea. But they don't want to immediately rush to introduce e-scooters to the city, as there could be unforeseen consequences. They decide to use *Change-mapping* to explore the issue **before** trying to resolve it.
The first mission will explore the Big-Picture of e-scooters in the city. As they proceed with the mission they also run a **Nested mission**. A Nested mission is usually run when investigating one issue uncovers another issue, which is connected to the first. If the connected issue is fairly simple, then the team could just use a tool, as shown in the next few pages. But in our example, the exploration prompts the team to look into how their organisation functions generally.

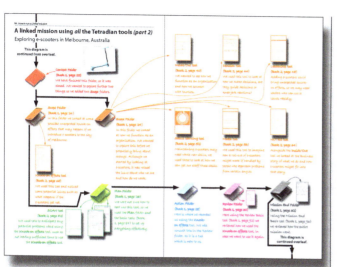

*Linked missions and Nested missions

These specialised missions are shown in the first Change-mapping book.
Page 36 Linked missions
Page 114 Nested missions

The first mission including the Nested mission is shown over two spreads, to allow you to see what is going on and why. At the end of that mission the team feel that introducing e-scooters to Melbourne *would* benefit all stakeholders. Therefore they run a second mission, linked to the first. This second mission runs exactly as before, but now the revised issue is: *How would they implement e-scooters into the city of Melbourne?*

At this stage they can still cancel the whole implementation as the second mission may show that although it is a good idea, it would not work for the city of Melbourne.

We see over the next two spreads how the team explore implementation further. Part of this involves using the **Service cycle** tool *(see page 30)* to better understand the customer's journey. The team are unsure how to best use this tool so instead of just using the tool, they set up a Scope folder to explore their options. They also use **Plan**, **Action** and **Review** folders to set up and record the using of the **Service cycle** tool. As in the first mission they use a Nested mission to explore in detail a different but connected part of the mission.

This chapter shows in simple detail, how to use all the tools in quite a complex mission and that *Change-mapping* follows a simple logic.

How to run large complex missions will be shown in much more detail in the upcoming book: *Advanced Change-mapping*, available soon.

A linked mission using *all* the Tetradian tools *(part 1)*
Exploring e-scooters in Melbourne, Australia

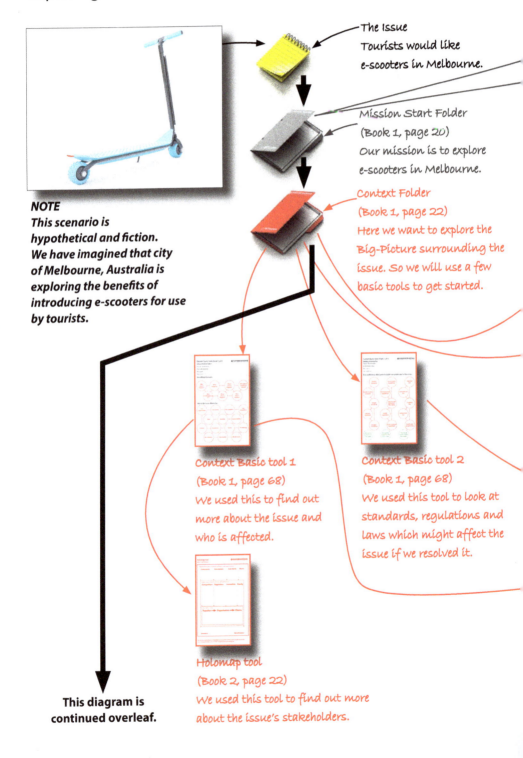

  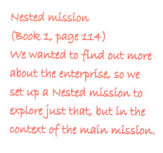

Mission Start Basic tool 1
(Book 1, page 62)
We used this tool to set up a mission to explore more about e-scooters in Melbourne, but NOT to start installing e-scooters in the city, now!

Mission Start Basic tool 2
(Book 1, page 62)
This tool acts like a map of the mission, showing where we are in the mission.

Nested mission
(Book 1, page 114)
We wanted to find out more about the enterprise, so we set up a Nested mission to explore just that, but in the context of the main mission.

 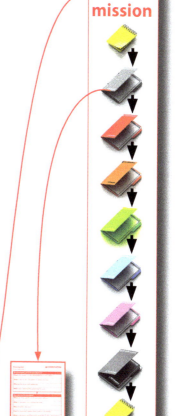

Context Basic tool 3
(Book 1, page 68)
We used this to find out what would take priority of and when we resolved the issue.

Context Basic tool 4
(Book 1, page 68)
We used this tool to look at how we would review how the issue was resolved, if we resolved it.

Sense-making tool
(Book 2, page 10)
We needed more detail about the issue so we used this tool.

Effectiveness tool
(Book 2, page 34)
We wanted to get more detail about effectiveness criteria within our organisation.

Visioning tool
(Book 2, page 14)
Inside the Nested mission we used the Visioning tool to define the enterprise (see page iv). This was done in the Context of the main mission already running.

A linked mission using *all* the Tetradian tools *(part 2)*
Exploring e-scooters in Melbourne, Australia

This diagram is continued from overleaf.

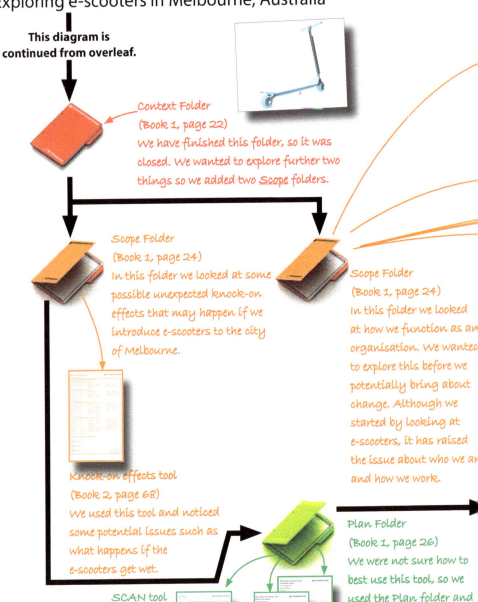

Context Folder
(Book 1, page 22)
We have finished this folder, so it was closed. We wanted to explore further two things so we added two Scope folders.

Scope Folder
(Book 1, page 24)
In this folder we looked at some possible unexpected knock-on effects that may happen if we introduce e-scooters to the city of Melbourne.

Scope Folder
(Book 1, page 24)
In this folder we looked at how we function as an organisation. We wanted to explore this before we potentially bring about change. Although we started by looking at e-scooters, it has raised the issue about who we are and how we work.

Knock-on effects tool
(Book 2, page 68)
We used this tool and noticed some potential issues such as what happens if the e-scooters get wet.

Plan Folder
(Book 1, page 26)
We were not sure how to best use this tool, so we used the Plan folder and the basic tools (Book 1, page 84) to set up everything effectively.

SCAN tool
(Book 2, page 82)
We used this to anticipate any potential problems while using the Knock-on effects tool, such as not having sufficient time to use the Knock-on effects tool.

Inside/Out tool
(Book 2, page 40)
We wanted to see how we function as an organisation and how we connect with tourists.

Decision tool
(Book 2, page 44)
We used this tool to look at how we make decisions, are they guide decisions or knee-jerk reactions?

Leadership tool
(Book 2, page 48)
Adding e-scooters could bring unexpected knock-on effects, so we may need leaders who can solve issues rapidly.

Skills learning tool
(Book 2, page 52)
Maintaining e-scooters may need whole new skills, we used these to look at how we can get our staff those skills.

Modes tool
(Book 2, page 56)
We used this tool to imagine how a roll-out of e-scooters might work if handled by people who approach problems from certain angles.

NOTES tool
(Book 2, page 64)
Alongside the Inside/Out tool we looked at the business story of what we do and how e-scooters might fit into that story.

Action Folder
(Book 1, page 28)
Here is where we recorded us using the Knock-on effects tool. We will consult this in the Review folder, as it is a tool which is new to us.

Review Folder
(Book 1, page 30)
Here using the Review Basic tool (Book 1, page 92) we reviewed how we used the Knock-on effects tool, in case we want to use it again.

Mission End Folder
(Book 1, page 32)
Using the Mission End Basic tool (Book 1, page 96) we reviewed how the entire mission went.

This diagram is continued overleaf.

96. *How to run a Linked mission*

A linked mission using *all* the Tetradian tools *(part 3)*
Exploring e-scooters in Melbourne, Australia

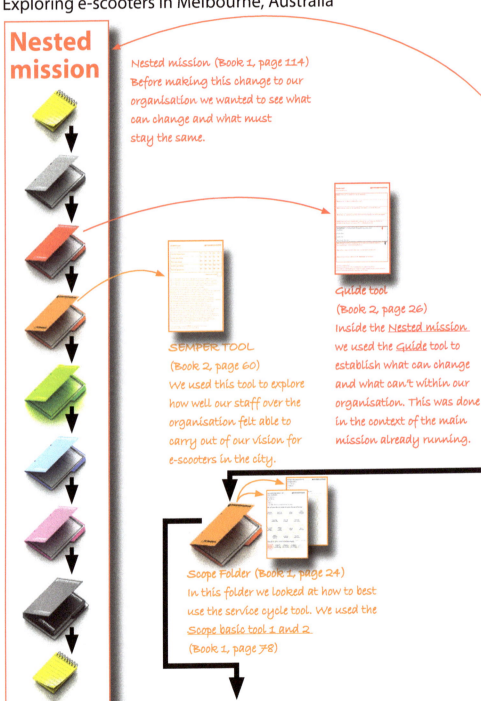

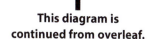
This diagram is continued from overleaf.

Mission End Folder
(Book 1, page 32)
At this stage we finished the first mission. We had found enough evidence to support introducing e-scooters to Melbourne. Now we wanted to explore how we would actually implement that.

The revised Issue —
How would we implement e-scooters into the city?

Mission Start Folder
(Book 1, page 20)
We set up a second mission to explore this issue using the basic tools. (Book 1, page 62)

Context Folder
(Book 1, page 22)
Here we want to explore the Big-Picture surrounding the revised issue. Most of it was the same as before, but we wanted more detail about the customer who would use the e-scooters.

Service cycle tool
(Book 2, page 30)
We wanted to use this tool to better understand the customer journey, but we were not sure how to best to use this tool.

Enterprise Canvas tool
(Book 2, page 18)
We used this tool to confirm how the e-scooters works and what we need to do to keep them running.

Value tool
(Book 2, page 6)
We used this tool to find out more what is valued by the customers while using the e-scooters.

98. How to run a Linked mission

A linked mission using *all* the Tetradian tools *(part 4)*
Exploring e-scooters in Melbourne, Australia

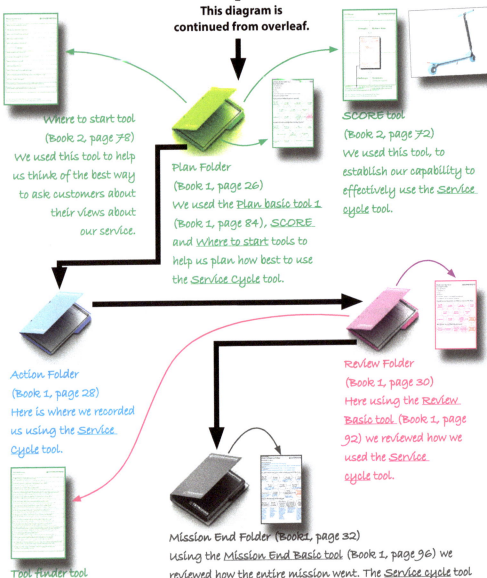

This diagram is continued from overleaf.

Where to start tool (Book 2, page 78)
We used this tool to help us think of the best way to ask customers about their views about our service.

SCORE tool (Book 2, page 72)
We used this tool, to establish our capability to effectively use the Service cycle tool.

Plan Folder (Book 1, page 26)
We used the Plan basic tool 1 (Book 1, page 84), SCORE and Where to start tools to help us plan how best to use the Service Cycle tool.

Action Folder (Book 1, page 28)
Here is where we recorded us using the Service Cycle tool.

Review Folder (Book 1, page 30)
Here using the Review Basic tool (Book 1, page 92) we reviewed how we used the Service cycle tool.

Tool finder tool (Book 2, page 86)
Although it is a Plan folder tool, we used this tool to find other review tools, such as an After Action Review tool.

Mission End Folder (Book 1, page 32)
Using the Mission End Basic tool (Book 1, page 96) we reviewed how the entire mission went. The Service cycle tool helped us better understand how to best implement e-scooters in Melbourne. So we now know that e-scooters would work well for our organisation, we now want to explore running an actual trial of e-scooters in the city.

A Linked mission using *all* the Tetradian tools *(part 4)*
The whole Linked mission

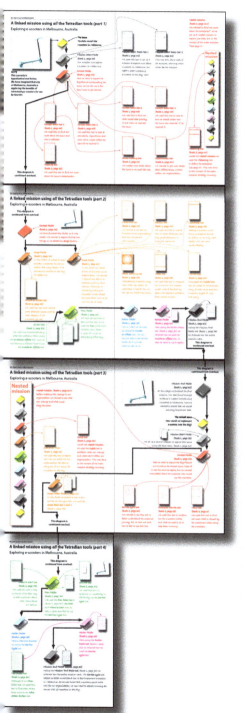

Overview
Here we see the last few pages joined together. We can see how the city of Melbourne used a Linked *Change-mapping* mission which was made up of two missions.

The first mission was exploring the issue of e-scooters in Melbourne. They wanted to find out more about the issue before trying to resolve it. They may have found that the issue didn't need resolving. If they had rushed to resolve it then this could have led to costly avoidable issues, further down the line.

The second mission looked at what implementing e-scooters might look like. Again not rushing to implement a new system without fully understanding everything, such as the customer journey.

We can see over the last few pages how the black line connects the folders and inside the folders are tools used to gather ideas, information and insights.

The city of Melbourne could end the mission at this stage or they could add a third mission to actually do the trail implementation of e-scooters in the city.

Finding out more
Chapter 3 and Chapter 12 of the first *Change-mapping* book go into more detail about larger missions and how you can use them to explore your issues.

Also the third book in this series *Advanced Change-mapping* book will show step by step how to run large complex missions to explore, resolve or address complex issues. See page 110 for more details about this upcoming book.

Chapter 5: Getting more out of *Change-mapping*
Some more ways to use these and other tools

NOTE
All the scenarios are hypothetical and fiction. The organisations mentioned are used to illustrate a specific issue to better describe how the tools could be used.

About this chapter
Throughout this book we have presented twenty new Tetradian tools to support the basic tools introduced in the first book *(see far right)*.

In this chapter we introduce some more ways to show what the tools and *Change-mapping* can do.

Using the tools in different scenarios
Inside the book we showed how each tool worked by using a scenario. In this part of the chapter *(see page 102)* we see how a tool can be used in *any* scenario, not only for a specific scenario. This allows you to fit the tool to your issue, rather than having to fit your issue to the tool.

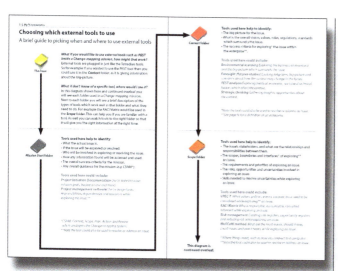

Adapting the tools to meet your needs
To be consistent we have shown all of the tools in this and the last book as being 22cm tall x 15cm wide and written in English. All the tools, some much more complex than others have been condensed to fit those proportions and language. But when you come to use the tools you may prefer the same tool four times the size and written in Spanish. In this part of the chapter *(see page 104)* we look more into this.

Choosing which external tool to use
This book has acted as an introduction to twenty Tetradian tools. *(Each tool also featured a link to more detailed information, available online on the authors weblog or other sites.)* But what if you either have an external tool but don't know how to incorporate it into *Change-mapping* or you want to find an external tool? This part of the chapter *(see page 106)* gives you a brief guide about choosing and using external tools within *Change-mapping*.

In brief
If you are not familiar with *Change-mapping* then it is worth reading through the first book which introduces *Change-mapping* and how to use it.

It is available at the time of writing on Amazon and other book retailers.
ISBN 978-1-906681-40-1

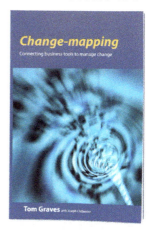

Using the tools in different scenarios
Adapting the tools for your needs

The scenarios
In the book we have used scenarios to show how these new tools can be used in *Change-mapping* missions. Each tool has been shown with a specific scenario, but the tools can be used in any scenario. For example the **Sense-making** tool *(see page 10)* was shown being used to help find lost meteorological data. Here we use the same tool *(see right)* in a different scenario: *A skills shortage in the Australian logistics industry*. The tool is used in exactly the same way as before.

Can I use the tools in isolation?
While of course the tools can be used in isolation, just like the fish in the image above, the tools are far more effective when they work together. There can be a temptation to rush to resolve an issue without fully understanding what the issue is. Using the tools as part of a mission will keep all stakeholders up to date with what they are doing and why.
This will be especially important when exploring or resolving large complex issues. If you have teams working on interconnected issues then this will avoid repetition and allow far better coordination.

Do the tools only work in one folder?
In this book we have shown the tools in specific colours, such as the red **Sense-making** tool *(see on the other page)*, indicating it is a **Context** folder tool.
Most of the tools can be used in other folders if required. For example the **Holomap** tool *(see page 22)* is also shown as a **Context** folder tool but it could be used in any of the other folders for example as a **Plan** folder tool.

Sense-making tool

CHANGE→MAPPING
CONNECTING BUSINESS TOOLS TO MANAGE CHANGE

Mission identification: Find why there is a skills shortage in the Australian logistics industry.

What is the issue?	**When** is it thought the issue occurs or occurred?	**Where** is it thought the issue occurs or occurred?
A skills shortage in the Australian logistics industry.	It is slowly happening as current drivers retire and no one to replace them.	The issue occurs across all Australia.
How is it thought the issue occurs or occurred?	**Who** is thought to be affected by the issue occurring?	**What** is it thought to cause the issue occurring?
The industry is seen to be a hard industry to work in with long hours and difficult conditions.	Companies trying to get goods hauled. Logistics companies can't haul goods.	Routes into the industry require licensing which can take time and seen as a tough job to do.
Why does the issue need resolving?	**What** apart from people is thought to be affected when the issue occurs?	**Why** is it thought the issue occurs?
A large percentage of Australian goods are moved by trucks across the country.	We are not sure.	The industry is not seen as glamorous as others in Australia with long hours and not much career progression.

Statement about the issue:

The current haulage drivers are approaching retirement age. While there is not enough new drivers coming into the industry due to licensing and some negative views about the industry.

This tool is adapted from a blog by Tom Graves:
http://weblog.tetradian.com/2018/03/14/sensemaking-into-the-void/

Adapting the tools to your needs
Different proportions and languages

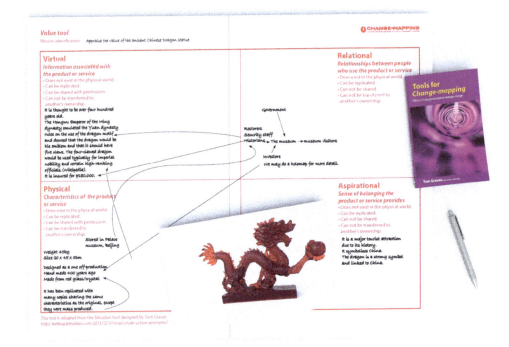

Different proportions
All the tools shown in this book have been designed to fit into the proportions of the book. But they can be adjusted to any dimensions required, for example a landscape **Value** tool *(see above)*. This will allow you to add more information while using the tool. In the example above the tool has gone from 22 cm x 15cm to 45cm x 66cm.

Different languages
The author has a vast network of contacts around the world. With this in mind the tools could easily be translated into other languages such as Spanish, as shown in the example on the other page *(see right)*. Here we see the **Holomap** tool which was designed by the author and Michael Smith while in Central America. We have shown the **Holomap** translated into Spanish. This can allow non-English speakers to still use the tools to help them explore and resolve issues.

To find out more about obtaining customised **Tetradian** tools email *info@tetradian.com*

Herramienta de holomapa

Identificación de la misión:

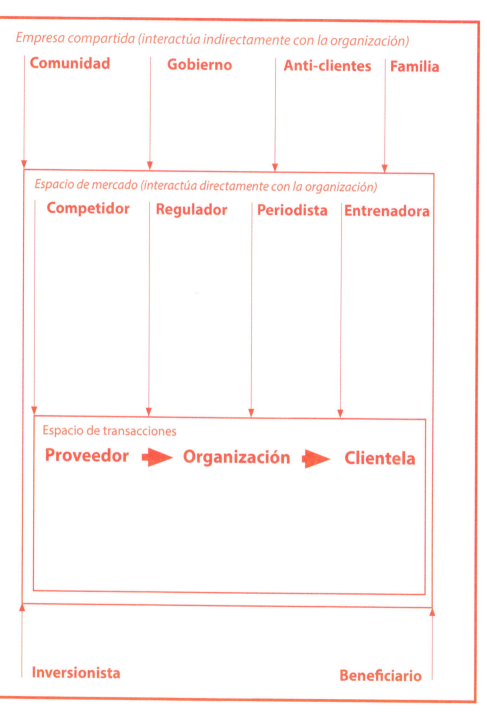

Esta herramienta está adaptada de la herramienta Holomap diseñada por Tom Graves y Michael Smith.
http://weblog.tetradian.com/2014/09/18/organisation-and-enterprise/

Choosing which external tools to use
A brief guide to picking when and where to use external tools

The issue

What if you would like to use external tools such as PEST inside a Change-mapping mission, how might that work?
External tools are plugged in just like the Tetradian tools. So for example if you wanted to use the PEST tool then you could use it in the **Context** folder, as it is giving information about the big-picture.

I don't know of a specific tool, where would I use it?
In this diagram shown here and continued overleaf you will see each folder used in a *Change-mapping* mission. Next to each folder you will see a brief description of the types of tools which work well in that folder and what they need to do. For example the RACI Matrix would be used in the **Scope** folder. This can help you if you are familiar with a tool. As well you can match tools to the right folder so that it will give you the right information at the right time.

Mission Start folder

Tools used here help to identify:
- What the actual issue is.
- If the issue will be explored or resolved.
- Who will be involved in exploring or resolving the issue.
- How any information found will be accessed and used.
- The overall success-criteria for the mission.
- Any overall guidance for the mission *(e.g. CSPAR)*.

Tools used here could include:
Project Initiation Documentation *Use to state the issue, mission goals, business-case and more).*
Project management software *Use to assign tasks, responsibilities, dependencies and resources while exploring, resolving or addressing the issue.*

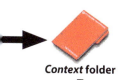

Context folder

Tools used here help to identify:
- The big-picture for the issue.
- What is the overall vision, values, rules, regulations, standards which surrounds the issue.
- The success-criteria for exploring, resolving or addressing the issue within the enterprise.

Tools used here could include:
Environmental scanning *Exploring the business environment and the big-picture which surrounds the issue.*
Foresight (futures-studies) *Looking long-term, big-picture and scenarios about how the context may change in the future.*
PEST analysis *Exploring political, economic, social and technical factors which affect the context.*
Strategic thinking *Gathering insights, opportunities about the context.*

Scope folder

Tools used here help to identify:
- The issue's stakeholders, and what are the relationships and responsibilities between them.
- The scopes, boundaries and interfaces of exploring, resolving or addressing an issue.
- The requirements and priorities of exploring an issue.
- The risks, opportunities and uncertainties involved in exploring an issue.
- Skills needed to resolve uncertainties while exploring an issue.

Tools used here could include:
VPEC-T *What values, policies, events, content, trust need to be considered while exploring an issue.*
RACI Matrix *Who is responsible, accountable, consulted, informed while exploring an issue.*
Risk management *Creating risk-registers, opportunity-registers, and reducing risk while exploring an issue.*
MoSCoW method *What are the must-haves, should-haves, could-haves and won't haves, while exploring an issue.*

This diagram is continued overleaf.

This diagram is continued from overleaf.

Plan folder

Tools used here help to:
- Define plans, tasks, schedules and resource-needs to explore an issue.
- Guide innovation and research while exploring, resolving or addressing an issue.
- Develop work-instructions and check-lists for tasks.
- Specify required information and information-capture.
- Marshal any resources required for tasks.

Tools used here could include:
Gantt Chart Use to plan tasks, schedules, resources and dependencies while exploring the issue *(or part of it)*.
Resource planning What materials, equipment, people, logistics are required to explore the issue.
Technology roadmap Use while planning to explore the issue, by matching technology to best explore that issue.
TRIZ Use to help explore complex problems and consider potential solutions to those problems.

Action folder

Tools used here help to:
- Guide activities within the task, as specified in the *Plan* folder, work-instructions, check-lists etc. You would use these while performing a task, such as performing an interview. These would help you anticipate problems, before they happen and act as guidance if the plan doesn't match reality.
- Capture information, ideas, insights, events and exceptions while exploring the task. For example if your task was to perform an interview, someone else would record the interview taking place. This would be viewed later to see if anything could be improved.

Other tools used here could include:
Exception handling Noting any exceptions to what usually happens, while performing a task.
Event logging The automated logging of activity and events while performing a task.

Review folder

Tools used here help to:
- Assess variances, insights and exceptions. Did what actually happened match what was meant to happen?
- Compare task-outcomes to success-criteria. Did you achieve what you wanted to achieve?
- Support quality-improvement and process-improvement if the task was repeated.
- Support skills-development, which will be of benefit should the task or similar tasks be repeated.

Tools used here could include:
After Action Review Use to review what happened, what could be improved and if the plan was followed, while performing a task.
Post-mortem documentation Use to record lessons-learned and project-outcomes after performing a task.
Benefits realisation management Use to assess if a task was executed successfully.
Incident management Use to analyse any incidents which happened while the task was executed and to reduce any risks if the task was to be repeated.

Mission End folder

Tools used here help to:
- Review outcomes of the overall mission. While a **Review** folder tool might review a part of a mission, a tool used here would review the entire mission.
- Support continuous-improvement. A **Review** folder tool might look at the improvement of a particular task inside a mission, here it would look at the improvement of all tasks inside a mission.

Tools used here could include:
Benefits realisation management Use to assess the success of a mission. Did the overall mission resolve or address the issue?
Change management Use to manage how change would affect and be implemented across an organisation.

Where can I find out more?
To find out more about a specific tool try Wikipedia to find out more. *(See the legal disclaimer at the start of the book)*.
This diagram can help you match your tools specifications with the ones shown here.
Also the **Tool finder** tool *(shown left)* can help you pick a tool which you are unfamiliar with, see page 86.

What's next in *Change-mapping*?

Advanced *Change-mapping*

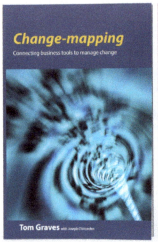

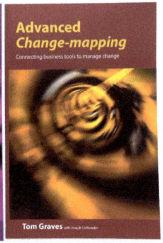

About the third book in the series

Advanced Change-mapping will show you how to tackle large scale, complex change issues. This book is aimed at people who are familiar with how *Change-mapping* works and now want to know more about the **why** of change-mapping as well as the **how**. The book will feature step by step guides, scenarios and in-depth analysis of the inner workings of advanced *Change-mapping*. Coming soon!

Future developments

Currently in development *(at the time of writing)* the author is developing training courses, apps and games based around Change-mapping and some of his other systems.

As a consultant based in Australia the author is available to work with organisations on change issues, for more information visit ***http://tetradian.com***

Find out more
www. changemappingbook.com
More information about *Change-mapping*.

http://weblog.tetradian.com/
A large collection of blog posts by the author about change issues and more.

Other books by the author

A selection of books about Enterprise architecture

About these books

The author has also written a large number of books which offer a more technical view of change and enterprise architecture. Some of the books also expand on the tools shown in this book. A selection of titles include:

The Service-Oriented Enterprise
This book explores how enterprise architecture and viable services link together to create a simpler yet far more powerful view of the enterprise, as a dynamic, unified whole.

The enterprise as story
This ground-breaking book places story at centre-stage for the architecture, itself using a narrative structure to explore the role of narrative in enterprise-architecture.

Doing enterprise architecture
This book provides a step by step guide to developing an enterprise architecture, guided by the stages of the well known CMMI maturity model.

To find out more visit:
www.tetradianbooks.com/

Glossary

Agile
Originally from software design, Agile uses adaptive planning, evolutionary development, early delivery, and continual improvement, and encourages flexible responses to change.

Anti-client
Anti-clients will not engage in transactions with you, they will actively reject engagement with you and your organisation – and incite others to do the same.

Backbone
Backbone adds *Agile* to *Waterfall* to take advantage of both methods. This would give a project flexibility without spiralling out of control.

Beneficiary
A person or group who will receive benefit from investing in an organisation or enterprise. Note this investment is not limited to financial investment.

Big Data
Big Data deals with data sets that are too large or complex to be dealt with by traditional data-processing software.

CRM
Customer relationship management *(CRM)* is the process of managing interactions with existing, past and potential customers.

CSPAR
Change-mapping uses a system called *CSPAR*. *CSPAR* splits an issue into **C**ontext, **S**cope, **P**lan, **A**ction and **R**eview folders. Inside each folder are tools used to gather information, ideas and insights.

Digital transformation
Digital Transformation replaces non-digital or manual processes with digital processes or replaces older digital technology with newer digital technology.

Disaster recovery
Disaster Recovery is a set of policies, tools and procedures to enable the recovery or continuation of vital technology infrastructure and systems following a disaster.

Enterprise
An organisation is *part* of an enterprise but it is not *the* enterprise. If we imagine a copper mine, their enterprise is to mine copper. Mining the copper involves a huge amount of individual issues which need to be resolved. This continual resolving of issues *is* the enterprise. Inside the enterprise will be the organisation, suppliers, customers, equipment and much more.
For more information see *www.slideshare.net/tetradian/the-enterprise-is-the-story/*

Enterprise Architecture

Enterprise architecture *(EA)* is concerned with the structures, behaviours and narrative of a business, in context of its broader enterprise.

Explorers

Explorers use *Change-mapping* missions to explore, resolve or address issues. They gather ideas, information and insights about the issue.

Interface

An interface *(in this book)* is where a customer or client has contact with an organisation's service or product. Such as a customer using a website.

Investor

A person or group who invests in an organisation or enterprise. Note this investment is not limited to financial investment.

Linked mission

A mission which is linked to one or more other missions, by sharing the same overall objective.

Mission

Change-mapping uses *missions* to explore, resolve or address issues. Missions use *CSPAR* to split the issue into manageable parts. A mission has a set of folders which contain tools used by *Explorers* to gather information.

Nested Mission

A *Nested mission* is a mission inside a larger mission. For example if you ran a mission to explore how to invest in a wind farm, you might also run a Nested mission about where you want your organisation to be in the future.

Observer

Observers are used in *missions* to record what the *Explorers* find in a mission. They are needed as often everyone will want to contribute ideas, but no one records the ideas.

Pathfinder

Pathfinders are used in *missions* to keep the *Explorers* on track and not lose focus, by *suggesting* the best tools to use to gather information.

Waterfall

Waterfall is a breakdown of project activities into linear sequential phases, where each phase depends on the deliverables of the previous one and corresponds to a specialisation of tasks.

Lightning Source UK Ltd.
Milton Keynes UK
UKHW022209050421
381481UK00007B/109

Enterprise Architecture

Enterprise architecture *(EA)* is concerned with the structures, behaviours and narrative of a business, in context of its broader enterprise.

Explorers

Explorers use *Change-mapping* missions to explore, resolve or address issues. They gather ideas, information and insights about the issue.

Interface

An interface *(in this book)* is where a customer or client has contact with an organisation's service or product. Such as a customer using a website.

Investor

A person or group who invests in an organisation or enterprise. Note this investment is not limited to financial investment.

Linked mission

A mission which is linked to one or more other missions, by sharing the same overall objective.

Mission

Change-mapping uses *missions* to explore, resolve or address issues. Missions use *CSPAR* to split the issue into manageable parts. A mission has a set of folders which contain tools used by *Explorers* to gather information.

Nested Mission

A *Nested mission* is a mission inside a larger mission. For example if you ran a mission to explore how to invest in a wind farm, you might also run a Nested mission about where you want your organisation to be in the future.

Observer

Observers are used in *missions* to record what the *Explorers* find in a mission. They are needed as often everyone will want to contribute ideas, but no one records the ideas.

Pathfinder

Pathfinders are used in *missions* to keep the *Explorers* on track and not lose focus, by *suggesting* the best tools to use to gather information.

Waterfall

Waterfall is a breakdown of project activities into linear sequential phases, where each phase depends on the deliverables of the previous one and corresponds to a specialisation of tasks.

Lightning Source UK Ltd.
Milton Keynes UK
UKHW022209050421
381481UK00007B/109